Don Alias

stories of a legendary percussionist

Melanie Futorian

Cover design & art work -Yoko Yamabe   *Photography - Melanie Futorian*

To my unique and most wonderful companion
and his children, Kimmi and Doni Jr.

Sketch by Don Alias

Foreword

It all started when I moved into apartment 3E, one wall apart from Don Alias. My new neighbor and I would talk endlessly in the hallway, which eventually led to an invitation for dinner. Don prepared his specialty of pasta, garlic salt, and ketchup, and over this meal, the countless musical stories began.

Music filled his every day, so it was natural that we established a rhythmic code on the wall. A Guaguancó meant "hey baby, I'm home," while another rhythm signified "come on over." He'd shake oatmeal or rice in the box, beat on pots and pans while preparing a meal, and even knock on a door as if it were a performance.

As his companion for eight years until his death, Don shared his musical and personal experiences with me. This book is derived from our many captivating conversations, his personal journal entries, as well as my time accompanying him on tour. To honor his memory, I felt compelled to document these stories that might otherwise be lost.

These intimate vignettes, often humorous and entertaining, recount Don's rise to prominence from humble beginnings. They record his collaboration with some of the most influential musicians of our time, including Dizzy Gillespie, Nina Simone, Miles Davis, Elvin Jones, Tony Williams, Jaco Pastorius, and Joni Mitchell. His love of music led to a fifty-year career in which he set a new standard in percussion in a multitude of musical genres from Afro-Cuban to jazz.

Prologue

My name is Don Alias and I was born on Christmas Day.

Where it really all began was with my grandmother, Rose. Someone has to have role models, icons, people whom they emulate. For me it wasn't a movie star, world leader or an athlete. It was my grandmother, the pillar and backbone of my family.

Rose was born and raised on the Dutch side of St. Maarten, a small island in the Lesser Antilles, which explained the occasional Dutch words and songs she sang to us. She had all those wonderful island qualities, such as dancing, singing and was a master of Caribbean cuisine. She was tall and statuesque with incredibly high cheekbones and deep brown skin. No question her values came from the old school such as hard work, strong morals and strength of character. She was a champion of the best education and obtained her high school diploma when she was well into her forties. And boy, was she strict!

Grandmother Rose was a great swimmer, different from many islanders who didn't swim. She sewed all her own clothes including her underwear. She made soda in the bathtub with syrup and seltzer water and later she and my grandfather were one of the first Black couples to own a brownstone in New York. She loved challenges, and one day her sense of adventure brought her to America.

My grandmother told me that upon arriving on Ellis Island, all the passengers had to wait in line with their papers to see doctors and be processed. It was easier for her than most travelers because as you probably know, West Indians speak English, though often misunderstood because of their lilting accent. Rose stood in line not knowing that the man behind her was in admiration of her beauty. His name was Samuel James Richardson and was from the island of Anguilla, which is close to St. Maarten. It was then that he decided he wanted to marry her.

Samuel noticed that Rose's address in New York was written on her suitcase. He jotted it down. They had a small conversation and a bit of a flirt before they left each other's company to be processed. The two went their way, but shortly after their New York arrival, Samuel walked from his home downtown in the 20's to where Rose was living uptown, which was quite a distance. He showed up at her doorstep to court her and they were married shortly thereafter.

Rose and Samuel had several children, one of whom was my mother, Violet. A generation later, my mom married a guy named Eugene, and my brother and I were born.

Table of Contents

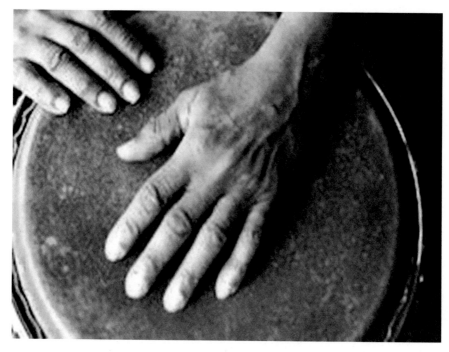

1.

In the Beginning with Eartha Kitt

I got started on the streets of New York City literally, but I'll get to that in a minute. I was born and raised in Harlem on 136th Street between 7th Avenue and Lenox in a brownstone owned by my grandparents. It was near the famous clubs Red Rooster Bar and Smalls Paradise, where slick numbers men like Walking Jack and Dapper Bob strolled the avenues in their clean, sharp and dap clothes.

We were a Black family in the neighborhood and because we were West Indian, we were known as "Geechies." My grandparents, who were from the island of St. Maarten, played Calypso music day in and day out. Calypso and R&B were everywhere. It was in the society dance halls, bars, and blared on the radios. Songs like Harry Belafonte's

"Matilda" and "Man Smart, Woman Smarter" were really hot during that time. I remember being eleven-years-old and pounding on pots and pans as my mother danced in the kitchen while she was cooking. It was peas and rice, fungi and okra with a treat of pig's feet for New Years. Somewhere down the line, I acquired a kind of Chinese drum and started to beat on it without really knowing about rhythm, just relying on natural feeling. By the time I was thirteen, I was hanging with the neighborhood kids playing music on the streets. Spider, Roach and I were on congas. Bumstead and my brother sang. Suffice to say that if I had to make a living with my voice, I'd be broke.

One day we were playing in the subway when a slick looking gentleman came up to us and said, "You guys sound good, why don't you come down to The Baby Grand? I want to give you a shot, a little spot." We were so excited, but we knew our parents wouldn't let us out of the house after nine o'clock, so my brother and I planned what we called "the great escape." After seeing all those westerns, detective stories and old spooky movies, we put pillows in the bed to resemble our bodies and then snuck out through the basement.

We were so proud to be leaving 136th Street and going down to 125th to play. All of our friends and the general neighborhood were wishing us well. I remember them saying, "Go ahead man, you all go on ahead." When we got down to 125th Street and knocked on the door of The Baby Grand, they told us to get the hell out of there. Of course we were too young to get into the club, but we hadn't given it much thought before then. So, we figured we'd set up in front of the club and make a little change. All I can remember is that I had my head

2

down beating on this drum and as I turned to the side, I saw the brigade coming. There were my grandmother and mother storming up the street in their nightgowns and my stepfather and grandfather in their pajamas and bathrobes close behind.

When my mother saw that my feet weren't sticking out from under the covers, she pulled back the sheets, saw the pillows and all hell broke loose. My grandmother, because she was the matriarch of the family, came over to me and very coolly sat down. In her West Indian lilt she said, "Give de boy de pump." I'm not sure where she got that word but she used to call my drums "de pump." I handed over my tambour to someone and I felt a solid whack of an umbrella across the side of my shoulder. At this point my brother and I decided we would run away because we were afraid of the punishment that was coming next for our dastardly deed.

I remember the scene because a crowd had gathered, including a few firemen who stopped by to see what had caused the commotion. Well, my mother lit into them and told them, in essence, to mind their own goddamned business because these were her kids and she could do what she wanted with them. It was quite embarrassing, but more so for our strict West Indian family to catch us outside playing. To them it was shameful, as if we were begging. They beat us all the way home.

My mother really discouraged me from playing. In fact, she had visions of me becoming a medical doctor, as you will find out. To this day, I'm not sure if she really realizes what I do. Of course, after that incident, I never should have ventured into playing music, especially "de pump," but here we go.

3

The next time I was uptown playing I was sure not to be caught. I was fifteen-years-old and at the YMCA on 135th Street playing for The Eartha Kitt Dance Society. A group of kids was learning African dance and I was their drummer. I didn't know anything about African music, not a thing. The dance studio reeked of sweat and oils and the dancers were wearing very little. They were moving across the floor matching the beat of my drumming.

Eartha Kitt walked in with two drummers. She was striking with cocoa-colored skin and eyes like a cat. Eartha began to command an exciting dance class accompanied by drummers Sonny Morgan and Juan Amalbert, who happened to be some of the best hand percussionists on the scene. As Eartha took the dancers across the floor, Juan and Sonny started to play and I tried unsuccessfully to play with them. Well, let's just say that I got my first baptism by fire because I had no idea what the hell they were doing. Sonny turned around and said, "Man, don't play, listen. Just listen." I stopped playing and listened intently. I was completely knocked out with all their patterns and rhythms, and thought I'd better get myself together quickly.

Eight months later, Eartha Kitt was headed to Newport to dance with Dizzy Gillespie's Big Band and picked me to go with her. I'd been attending an all-White, Catholic high school where no one had even heard of Eartha or Dizzy. I felt worlds apart from my classmates. Man, I was going to play with Dizzy Gillespie's Big Band at the Newport Jazz Festival. What an incredible honor. By the time she chose me, I had already gotten more experience playing Afro-Cuban

4

music, but nothing compared to the talent and knowledge of the other drummers. Maybe she saw something in my playing that was interesting. Well, it didn't go over too well with those drummers that Eartha had selected me. They didn't like it at all. They took offense to the point of cornering me in the street one day and threatened me. They were saying things like, "Who do you think you are?" and "What are you doin'?" All I could do was look at them sympathetically and say, "Hey, you know, that's just the way it is."

Eartha Kitt, the catwoman herself, drove me to the Newport Jazz Festival. I had to beg my mother to let me go, as to have a son beatin' on drums was really taboo for a middle class, Black family. I guess Mom thought that this was a passing thing, so not taking it too seriously, she finally approved.

Driving up to Newport, we first stopped in Connecticut to visit one of Eartha's friends who lived on some huge estate. We drove up a really long road and then some more to an enormous house. Inside was an afternoon party and after socializing a bit, we all sat down to eat. I had no exposure to anything beside my mother's West Indian cooking, and the Lobster Thermidor and champagne they served was a foreign subject altogether. It was rich and creamy with sauces and butter and stuff. After overeating and saying goodbye, we continued on to Newport only to stop shortly thereafter for me to throw up all over Eartha's dark blue car. It was my first gig and already I was off to an embarrassing start. Eartha though, was sympathetic. We finally reached the festival and to my amazement, my idols George Shearing and Billie Holiday, were on the bill with Dizzy. Fortunately, Dizzy had picked out some of his Afro-Cuban music for the gig, so I knew exactly what to play. He was one of the first musicians to incorporate Afro-Cuban music into his compositions and had hired premier percussionist Chano Pozo to perform with him. He and Chano wrote a great deal of Afro-Cuban music and it was this music that he chose for Eartha's dancing. I'd listened to his music ever since I was young - songs like "Manteca," "Tin Tin Deo" and "Con Alma." I didn't have any problem playing them, and man, it was wonderful performing in that band. There was also an eighteen-year-old trumpet player named Lee Morgan along with Wynton Kelly and Charlie Persip.

Eartha Kitt was dancing and definitely something with her dancer's body, but I was hardly looking at her 'cause I was so involved in the music. It was great. You can see the whole extravaganza in a New York Times photograph, the first Sunday in July 1957. I was sitting in the back wearing a suit and you can see the fear and excitement in my eyes. It was all a bit overwhelming.

Back in Harlem, I had plenty to tell the guys. I continued going to the Calypso dances at the famed Renaissance Ballroom on 138th Street. Fats Greene and a guy named Macbeth led the band and we were shakin' it up on the dance floor to his latest Caribbean inspired hits. I also frequented the Apollo and loved it there 'cause the acts were so diverse. You could hear such great jazz musicians as Thelonious Monk, Count Basie and Art Blakey along with Tito Puente, Tito Rodriguez, Machito and others in the Latin idiom. The Dominos, Frankie Lyman and The Teenagers and The Dells took care of the rhythm and blues, or as it was known on the block, doo-wop. On the comic side there was Pigmeat Markham and Moms Mabley, who could literally make you wet your pants laughing. If this wasn't enough, there'd be dance acts such as Pegleg Bates, The Mambo Aces and The Katherine Dunham Dance Troupe, that occasionally had a great conga player play named Julio Collazo. He was a cat who was very highly regarded in the Santeria religion. We'd watch him cop those rhythms and then we'd go right out and buy a new album like "Puente and Percussion" which was just percussion and bass. Man, if you want to know about playing conga drums and Latin music, you've got to know about that record.

Cachao had just come out with his "Descarga" album. He'd created a bass line that everybody was humming, and boy, did he have a great lineup on that album. Guillermo Barreto played timbales and Tata Guines turned everybody out with his conga playing. Tata played with a sound and speed like nobody else. He was an absolute monster. Just one night at the Apollo would satisfy your musical jones and more often than not you'd meet up with your buddies from the block.

It was such a culturally fruitful time and my brother and I were so inspired by all these great cats that we joined a Latin-jazz band. We played songs like Cal Tjader's "Night in Tunisia" and "Masacote." We'd play those tunes in 6/8 rhythms all night long and then listen to Willie Bobo and Mongo Santamaria to work out the breaks. I thank the lucky stars that I got this varied musical education. It helped me later on when I could adapt these different styles of music to my playing. Life was so much fun then, listening to these great performers, playing music, getting dressed up fine and going out in the ever-frustrating pursuit of girls. If you could dress really sharp and sing a little, then you could cop the babes more easily than those who couldn't. Times haven't changed all that much, have they, eh?

My brother Freddie and I were inseparable and we'd venture out to The Sugar Bowl on the corner of 138th and 7th. That's where all the college kids would hang, especially the ones courting and sparking fine, sepia beauties. It was the place to take them 'cause the jukebox was stocked with all the current jazz and rhythm and blues. It was there that I first heard "Round Midnight" performed by Miles Davis. We couldn't wait to swoon and slap each other five when Coltrane came in with his tenor sax solo. Then we all bought the Miles LP with *The Prince of Darkness* brooding on the cover with his shades. We loved his coolness as well as his music. One went hand in hand with the other. Those were definitely the days, my friend.

I learned how to play and sing along with George Shearing's piano solo on "Lullaby of Birdland" note for note and the guys on the block loved me for that. It was a learning period, a growing period for me, but before too long it was time for me to go away to college and learn something altogether different. Mom didn't want me to become one of those pride wrecking, financially unstable, "No, not my son," disappointing musicians (what secretly everyone deep down inside would like to be). She wanted me high on the ladder of bragging rights with lawyers and dentists. She wanted her son to have one of those gold-plated professions, which gave family, and even friends of the family, enormous neighborhood prestige. She knew that I possessed something visually valuable to Blacks and Whites at that time.

It was so important that it determined what kind of job you'd get, your popularity, what parties you'd be invited to and what girls you could date. It even decided what apartments you could rent. Spike Lee depicted what I was in his movie. It was a god-awful, dumb racial concept, but I was the perennial light-skinned Negro. Mom saw that I had all the makings for having sure-fire success in the Black community. It was decided, she was going to replace my congas with a stethoscope, and was sending me off to school to become a doctor.

2.

College Days

With the end of summer came the end of hanging with the boys on the block, flirting with those sassy girls at the dance hall, and definitely what seemed like the end of good music. I said goodbye to my friends, Carl, Dale, and Chris, jealous of the fact that they'd be in New York coppin' all the hip rhythms. Unfortunately, I was going away to Gannon University in Erie, Pennsylvania and what the hell was up there? I had applied to a number of schools, but this was the one that gave me a scholarship for basketball. I was a pretty fair basketball player. My six-foot-four frame didn't hurt and I had a damn good jump shot from the top of the key. So, I guess I was going there, thirteen miles from Canada and cold as hell. It was an all-boys, Catholic school run by Jesuits and I was sure that no one knew anything about Afro-Cuban or Latin rhythms.

Mom had warned me that no way could I take my conga drums. "You nuts, you want to take your conga drums up there? You got to be kidding! You're going to study, boy," she said vehemently. Come hell or high water, she was going to make me into that doctor, so I was going to Gannon to study pre-med.

I don't even remember my dad giving me a farewell. He split the day after he was supposed to be watching my brother and me. He left us toddlers alone in the house and that didn't go over very well with my mother. When Mom returned, she was so mad she called my uncle and he ended up hanging my father out of the window by his feet. I guess that was enough to get him on his way. That plus my mother finding out he was making the rounds with all the pretty women around the block.

My brother Freddie was now on his own, starting to become a junkie and clearly hanging out with the wrong crowd. He was lost in his own world and his musical potential fell by the wayside when he started getting high. Freddie was initially so serious when it came to his music that I remember him kicking the female piano player in the behind for messing up when he was playing a solo. She later became his girlfriend. Hey, maybe she liked being kicked in the ass.

Well, back to my farewell. Fortunately, I had taken a few jazz albums with me like Miles Davis, "Round Midnight," "The Night at Birdland," "HIP," "Poinciana," and some of Art Blakey and the Jazz

11

Messengers, and Ahmad Jamal. I got to school and my roommate, Jess Farlow, eventually got hooked on jazz after listening to all of my albums. And just as I thought, no one knew anything about Afro-Cuban or Latin music. Besides, where you gonna find a conga in Erie?

Once on the basketball court I felt at home with everything except the team, the students and the coach. The coach was definitely prejudiced and not even a good coach at that. Initially he made it hard for me to make the team. He had an attitude with me, though he treated everyone else with enthusiasm. It could have been that I was the only Black student and he, as well as everyone else, was White. He made it clear that he didn't like my color. To add to the insult, the gym floor was made out of concrete, not wood. Of course the positive thing was that when we got to play on wood, we could jump like hell. He saw that I made a great outside shooter since I was tall and I became the first five. Believe me, it wasn't fun because of the coach. He had that hostility so typical of racists.

Then one night, when we were supposedly tucked away in our dorms, I snuck out in an effort to protest the basketball coach. Because it was a Catholic school with so-called morals, they felt it was immoral to criticize him. Well, I got some spare clothes and filled them up with newspaper making it into a dummy of the coach. Then Jess and I ran through the center of town with that raggedy dummy. I called up the newspaper and informed them why I did it, not identifying myself. I got caught. They wrote about it and identified the caller as having a New York accent. I think they wanted to say Black accent. They asked us to confess or our whole floor would be punished. So, I admitted it and was grounded. I wasn't allowed to leave the premises after classes for three months. Around that time I really got acquainted with prejudice. I went to pledge the fraternities that my fellow basketball players were in and was denied. They didn't allow Jews and they didn't allow Blacks. I went to the Dean and protested and he said that the charter of the school originated down South and that they hadn't gotten around to changing it. It was 1959, before the Black revolution.

Dissatisfied and really missing music, I thought I'd try my hand at bass but didn't know a damn thing about that instrument. All I knew was how to play the line to the old Peter Gunn television theme. With that, I happened to get into a band and we played all the college functions. We ended up performing for the homecoming dance at Niagara University where the main attraction was Ahmad Jamal. He had Israel Crosby and Vernell Fornier, and we had to play after them. I looked at Israel Crosby playing that bass and I felt like a damn fool. I played bass in between my college studies, but things at school were still rough. The only other Black kid, a great basketball player, had already dropped out. We definitely had a little segregation problem, you know, and a couple of remarks were made to me. That was the last straw and I decided to get the hell out of that place and left school.

I actually bumped into my old roommate, Jess, thirty-three years later, when he showed up at one of my concerts with David Sanborn. He'd been following my career all those years and had ended up as a clothes salesman. Now it was time for me to rethink my education 'cause Gannon and I were just not getting along.

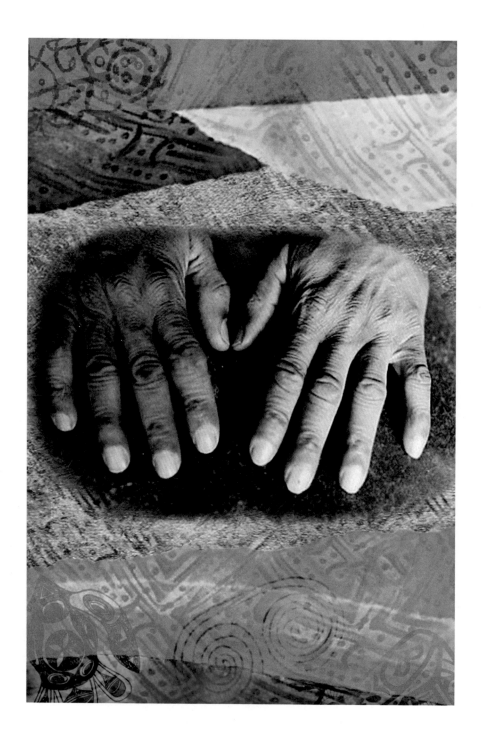

3.

Boston Days with Bill Fitch/Chick Corea
Gene Perla/Dick Meza

So I'm saying to myself, what's the next best thing to being a doctor? Well, working in a laboratory so I'd know what was wrong with the patients before the doctor did. I chose a small school up in Boston called Carnegie Institute specializing in biochemistry and laboratory analysis and was doing really well in my classes. I took chemistry, hematology, urinalysis, histology and general laboratory procedures. I couldn't get the music out of my head and ended up writing an essay in English class on how to construct a conga drum.

14

Funny enough, my teacher even gave me an A+ for that.

Mom was completely shattered that I wasn't going to be a doctor, but at least I was going to school that had something to do with medicine. I was living close to the Boston Commons near the Ritz Carlton with two Black roommates, and jazz was hot then in that city. It was around 1960 and the Schillinger House on Newbury Street had just become Berklee College of Music. Quincy Jones had split but Herb Pomeroy was there. Alan Dawson was teaching around the corner from a hotel called 905, which had a great reputation, 'cause legends like Charlie Parker and Thelonius Monk had stayed there. But I didn't even have a conga drum, since I was going to study biochemistry and work in a lab, you remember? I did work in a lab in no time though. Just picture, I'm in the middle of all these great musicians wearing white scrubs all day long.

One day I was walking down the street with a classmate of mine, when a guy popped out of the Berklee dormitory. He had the most un-Cuban, un-Spanish name; Bill Fitch, the same name as the Boston Celtics coach. He came up to me and said, "Do you know anyone who plays Latin percussion?" Now we're talking about magic, ladies and gentlemen, magic, and I said. "Yeah, man, I do." I thought he was just fooling around but then Bill said to me, "Come on upstairs, man, I got some conga drums."

By this time I'd acquired even more knowledge of Afro-Cuban music like Bembes and such and also some Haitian rhythms. We went upstairs and he sat down and started to play. Oh boy, I thought, here's a colleague and a friend. I could really relate to his talent. We caused

15

such a racket that someone was pounding the hell out of the door. It was the head of the dormitory at the time, Arif Mardin, who later became an executive with Atlantic Records.

We had to stop, but our deep musical friendship and our relationship as brothers had started. Bill was one of the few percussionists I'd ever met who could not only compose but also notate music. He later joined Cal Tjader's band taking Changuito's place, another great conga player. If you're a conga player, let me tell you, go to the archives and get that record by Cal Tjader. Bill wrote a tune on that album that's the epitome of a classic, classic conga drum solo.

One night, I was walking around Cambridge with my conga drum looking for somewhere to play. Harvard Square happened to have little dark cafes where Jack Kerouac and Allen Ginsberg types would hang. They'd be reciting beatnik poetry and playing flutes and I'd accompany them with my congas. I came across this famous jazz spot named Club 47. I peered in and saw this boy sitting behind a set of drums. I couldn't believe how young he looked. He couldn't have been more than fifteen or sixteen but man was he swinging! That amazing drummer was Tony Williams. Need I say more? A guy by the name of Leroy Falana was playing piano and Phil Morrison was on bass and I just wanted to sit in. I was starved for playing and needed to do something more. Finally I ran into some guys who were interested in the same kind of music that I was and we got a group together. Pretty soon, I met Stanley Pinkney, Motongo and also Dick Meza, who became a good friend.

We played our Afro-Cuban sounds in coffee houses like Café Alhambra wearing suits and ties. At that time, being clean, wearing a suit and tie and playing in a club was hot. Meanwhile, I was still going to school and finances got real tight. I didn't want to call home for money 'cause I was a little too proud, so I moved from Commonwealth Avenue to Massachusetts Avenue. That meant a lower standard of living, but I got a room with Bill. We brought our congas and I set up equipment for my laboratory studies. Life was full of Afro-Cuban music and hematology. Believe it or not, when we played out, a good crowd always gathered to hear our Latin music and man, I actually wore those ruffled Xavier Cugat shirts!

Bill and I had a gig with a piano player, a young guy by the name of Chick Corea, who was about eighteen at the time. Oh boy, he had all those greats down, people like Wynton Kelly and Bill Evans. He knew what to do as far as jazz was concerned, but he hadn't been exposed to Latin music so we said, "Chick, why don't you listen to some of these records, you know?" Bill played his LPs of Tito Puente, Eddie Palmieri, Cal Tjader, Lonnie Hewitt and Vince Guaraldi, a great Latin jazz keyboard player from the West Coast. Lo and behold, the next day on the gig Chick sounded like Rene Hernandez. Not exactly like him, of course, but he had the concept down. The love was in his bones, his blood. In that way, he was a lot like me.

We got to the point where we were playing Latin music six nights a week. I did that for about two or three years and that club was always jammed. We changed personnel and a guy named Gene Perla started to play with us. We hit it off so well that he's remained my best friend for over forty years. Gene and I experimented with shall we say, multiple ways of taking mescaline and marijuana. You name it, we did it and we took all of it. In the meantime, I was listening to all kinds of records and started to play a little jazz. Guess what I started to play in that band? Gene's four-string bass. Chick wanted to play tunes like "All the Things You Are" and "Night in Tunisia" and my ear was good enough to be able to make those changes. Gene was a terrific musician and an accomplished keyboard player and man, he could get bit. When he heard Charlie Haden hit some of those bottom notes on an Ornette Coleman record, he decided to play bass. The good thing about that band was that we all switched off instruments, but most of the time Mark Levine played trombone, Gene played piano and I played bass because I had learned to read a little bit of signature key changes.

Then Chick decided to leave Boston. He was headed to New York and one of his first gigs was with Mongo Santamaria. Dick Meza and I were the nucleus of the band, but all of a sudden Dick came and said, "Listen, I'm gonna go to New York." Gene and I tried to keep the band going. After Dick left, we had a saxophone player, Don Garcia, who was a bit of an avant-garde player, but Salsa music wasn't really his thing. Then Gene decided he was leaving for New York 'cause he wanted to play with Elvin Jones and I was the only one left.

During that period, I'd gotten married to a spunky gal named Paulette and we had our first kid, Doni, Jr. I loved them, but they were suffering 'cause I was delving into the drug scene. You know, it was acid time and I was taking acid. I was living a split life of music, family and biochemistry. I was working in a terminal hospital in Cambridge.

In other words, a patient went in with cancer and never came back out. Gene and I stayed in close contact and he told me he'd landed a gig with Nina Simone. Man, what a great gig. To make ends meet, I was playing at some local clubs and using an old drum set Gene had lent me. A few years later, my second baby came along, a beautiful girl named Kimberly Marisa Alias, who today remains as beautiful as ever.

The Boston Strangler was prowling around Boston and I put three locks on my apartment door to protect my family and called them on every break. I wasn't making any money, maybe ninety-five dollars a week and giving ninety to the household. I was trying to exist on five dollars and trying not to ask Mom for money, since, you know, she never approved of my music. I landed a really good research job in oncology at the Rhode Island Hospital and relocated my wife and kids to Providence. I started playing some gigs in Boston with a band called Brass '68 with John Abercrombie, Peter Donald, Rick Laird (who later went on to join Mahavishnu Orchestra), and Michael Gibson. Michael later did the scoring for the Broadway show "Grease" and asked me to be involved in the musical, but I wasn't able to do it.

I was commuting back and forth between Boston and Providence. In other words, I worked at the lab from nine to five, slept for maybe an hour; got on the bus to Boston, started the gig at nine and finished about one; caught the bus back to Providence around two-thirty; slept for a little while, and went to my day job at the lab. The hospital gig was really beautiful 'cause I had my own laboratory and I got to set up all of the procedures, but boy was I tired. I was doing a little coke on the side and you know how coke quickly catches

19

up with you. And if you don't know, then believe me, it really does.

One day I went to the laboratory and had some test tubes in my hand when all of a sudden I decided this was it, I was gonna go for it. I wrote my superior a letter saying that I was pursuing another occupation and then I split.

Around '67, some people out in California had promised me a gig with Johnny Martinez, who had a semi-Latin jazz sound. I picked up to move my family to California, but I made one fatal mistake. I stopped in New York for a couple of weeks to say goodbye to Mom before heading out. While I was in the city, I went to hear some music at the Salsa clubs. You know, everyone I'd been missing like Eddie Palmieri, Ricardo Ray and Tito Puente. The city was full of such great musicians. Man, I just had to stay in New York, so I sent my family back to Providence, Rhode Island.

I have to thank Paulette. She let me go. "Go ahead and be the musician you need to be," She said. She raised my children beautifully and endured hardships, so that I could be the person I became. I felt badly but it was just something I had to do. It's a hard thing to explain but I had no choice in the matter. Like I said, the music was in my blood, my bones.

You now know that I wasn't born Latin and my closest association to Latin America was the Caribbean. I didn't speak Spanish either but I still had an affinity for the music. I was frequenting the after-hour joints, which means the gig didn't start until three in the morning. All the guys showed up wearing their tuxedos and suits from their gigs earlier in the night. I really started to pay some dues doing that Cuchifrito Circuit. But what is Cuchifrito you might ask? Well, literally in Puerto Rican dialect, it's a meat dish with yellow corn meal fried to a golden brown. It's prevalent in Latin restaurants all over but especially in the barrios where the food is "down home." But in musical terms the Cuchifrito Circuit refers to those nightclubs that deal primarily with Latin music. In New York there were a slew of them up in the Bronx and in Spanish Harlem. Names such as The Palladium, Colgate Gardens, The Latin Palace and a very famous or infamous one depending on whether you got paid or not called the Tropicana. What made this club so special was that it produced some of the best Salsa in the world. It also was the meeting place for the most renowned musicians of the time. We're talking about Tito Puente, Patato Valdes, Ray Barretto, Ricardo Ray, Pacheco, Larry Harlow and Frankie Malabe.

One elite musician with whom I had the pleasure of playing was known in the inner circle as Kako. He was by far one of the unsung heroes of New York's underground musicians. He was a timbalero (a timbale player) of unmatched skill who played with such fire and flair. Certainly, many would agree he was on the same level as Tito Puente. What made the Tropicana so unique was that it was a great social playground for musicians. It was a place that they could go, relax and unwind after their own respective gigs.

As mentioned, it didn't open until three and the place started to rock about four or four-thirty. And I mean smoke! I had the honor of being one of the few non-Latin musicians invited to play onstage with the Latin cream of the crop. It was one of the great learning venues of all time. You really had to have some shit together or you'd be intensely

21

embarrassed in front of everyone to no end.

Getting into the club was no problem, however getting past the lines to the bathroom was another story. There were lines everywhere, to the bathroom and on the mirrors 'cause around that time cocaine was the drug of choice. Consequently, the bathroom was a choir of broken English and barrio Spanish along with loud sniffing and the blowing of noses. Naturally, the volume of the club increased as the night grew longer.

All the best and the baddest Latin musicians would come and sit in, and that was taken very seriously. I played timbales in the band with Kako as the leader and sometimes Patato would join us. Yeah! There was one guy that came in dressed in a tuxedo carrying a trumpet case. He walked on stage and placed it down with great care. He opened it elegantly, reached in and pulled out a cowbell along with a stick. He wailed on that cowbell, bringing that band to a whole other level. Maybe you might not have gotten paid for the night but you had a whole different kind of wealth in the Cuchifrito Circuit.

Gene Perla had landed a gig playing with my idols Willie Bobo and Patato Valdes. I went to watch Patato with Machito's great rhythm section, which included cats like Jose Mangual. Even to get close to them was a pleasure for me. I had always thought in terms of forward clave, you know, 2-3 as opposed to 3-2. I wasn't hip to the reverse clave as of yet, but I had the feel and soon thereafter started playing timbales too. Cal Tjader came into town and somehow or another I got into his circle. Cal had a gig at Colgate Gardens playing opposite a Latin-Jazz band with the sixteen-year-old Jerry Gonzales in it.

I can remember Armando Peraza saying to me, while Jerry was taking a solo, "Alias, that's a solo. Now when I play, I'll show you repertoire." And you know something? He sure did.

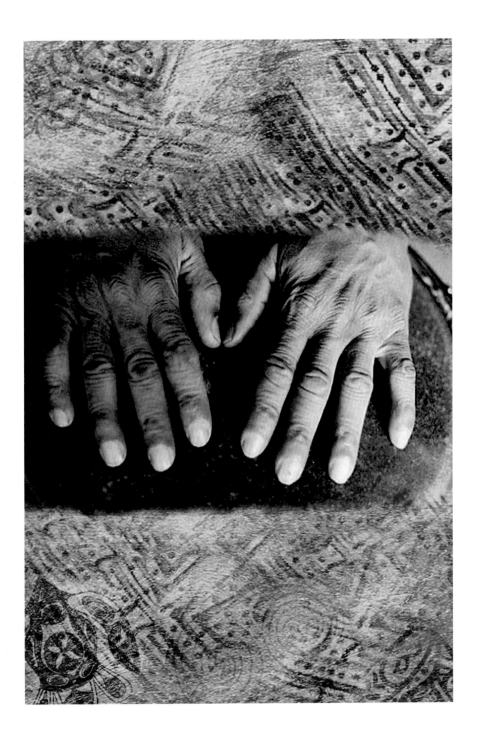

4.

Nina Simone

It was Gene Perla who called me up one day and said, "Hey man, why don't you just try to do this gig with Nina Simone?" I said, "Wow! Nina Simone, are you kidding?" At that time I was fearless. Play drums with Nina Simone? Sure. I remember our first gig was in New England somewhere. We were supposed to have rehearsal since I was new to the band. The band was still waiting for Nina when the audience began to walk into the concert hall. She came in so late that the actual rehearsal was the gig. When Nina walked in she really looked at me. You know, she looked me up and down and right through me. Here I was, this brown skinned, non-African-looking guy. It was at a time though when everyone wore dashikis and Afros, even the White guys. She had asked all her band members to wear an African medallion, so there I was in my black dashiki, semi-Afro and a glittering continent around my neck. Nina asked me where I was born and I replied, "On 136th Street and 7th Avenue in Harlem." There was no response. Then she just started telling me what she wanted to hear musically. She said, "In this first tune you're gonna play this and in the second you're gonna play that" and on and on. She counted off the first tune and we rolled into the set smoothly. Of course, by the time we got to the third tune it was all a blur and I'd forgotten what the hell she had said. I was just playing on gut feeling. She stood on the stage and called out, "Let's play in a different key." She'd actually do this and we'd have to transpose on the spot. Then she'd sing protest and Black revolutionary songs with her deep, earthy voice. After I finished playing, she looked at me and said, "You know somethin'? You're Blacker than you look." Of course, that was supposed to be a compliment. I really had to think about that comment over the years.

My grandfather was White, so my father looked like a dark Italian and I have features that are not necessarily Black, Black features. I think Nina was associating your soul and your ability to play Black music with the way you looked. She was involved with the Black Revolution so everything for her was Black oriented. How you carried yourself and what you wore somehow determined how Black you were.

25

It was something I never really paid too much attention to because who you were was all inside, you know.

I never thought that I'd ever get the chance to play in Europe, but a few months later here we were, Gene Perla, Weldon Irvine, Al Schackman and myself with Nina Simone. Our first stop was Dublin, where the streets were cobblestoned and there was a lot of green everywhere. There I learned how to play heavy and loud. For the first time I learned the true meaning of "dynamics of music" and the true meaning of a good, dark Lager beer. When we played for these audiences you could hear a pin drop. It was just a wonderful experience covering everything from, "Black is the Color of my True Love's Hair" to what she was most famous for, Gershwin's, "I Love You, Porgy." She would also perform songs written by politically motivated songwriters like Bob Dylan. We would do this song, "West Wind," written by Miriam Makeba, and before I took my solo, Nina would say, "Drums are like your heartbeat and you know you can't live without your heartbeat." That phrase had a special meaning to me that even today, I use as my motto.

Just as wonderful was that Miles Davis opened up for us. Anyway, I was playing "West Wind" when I caught Miles staring at me from offstage. I felt kind of nervous and kept wondering why he was staring so intensely. You have to keep in mind that Miles had always been my hero, my idol, and now this man was watching me. I found out later that Nina had gone over to the side of the stage and said to somebody, "I hope Miles Davis doesn't steal my drummer." But he did, of course.

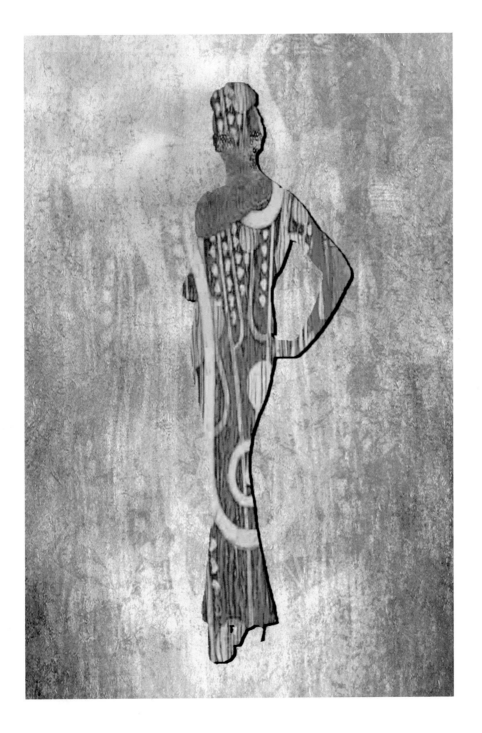

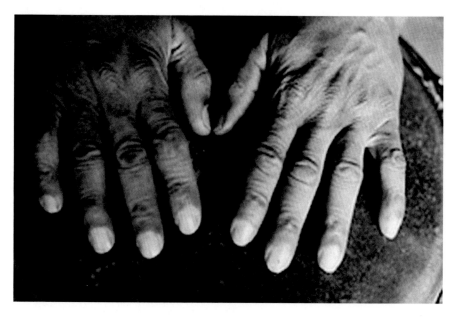

5.

Miles Davis

Lo and behold, we're talking '69 when I got the call from Tony Williams who said, "Miles is gonna do a really, monumental album and wants you to play on it." Man, when I walked into the studio and saw the "Bitches Brew" personnel, I knew it was going to be amazing. There was a percussionist friend of mine, Jumma Santos, whose name was really Jimmy Riley who I'd gotten on the gig with Nina Simone. Somehow or other he got himself on the session. Jack DeJohnette and Lenny White were on drums, Dave Holland and Harvey Brooks on bass, Bennie Maupin on bass clarinet, John McLaughlin on guitar and Wayne Shorter on sax. Chick Corea played keyboards with Joe Zawinul and Larry Young and I knew from the first note that it was going to change musical history and everyone's concept of Miles.

Everyone loved Miles' ballads like "My Funny Valentine." Oh, he played so pretty on those, but here comes "Bitches Brew," a potpourri of conjured up rhythms, sounds, textures and different electronics and thank God, Miles wanted to use percussion.

The "Bitches Brew" session lasted three days starting around ten in the morning. I ended up playing regular drums on "Miles Runs the Voodoo Down." I'd been practicing a drum rhythm that Gene Perla had shown me while I was living with him. It was actually Chris Hills, a great bass player who was friends with Gene, who had taught him that rhythm. It was a New Orleans funky kind of rock and roll beat and I had it down. Miles called "Miles Runs the Voodoo Down," but the drummers weren't getting it, which caused a little fraying of nerves in the studio. Miles called it again and on the third try he stopped it. Until then, every tune had been a first take. Everyone got a little nervous and I was sitting there saying to myself that Gene's rhythm would be just perfect for the tune. I took it upon myself to say, "Wait a minute, Miles, I got a rhythm for you that would be great for this tune." People started shuffling, looking around at each other waiting to see how Miles would react to this new guy. Miles just looked over and directed me to the drum tier telling me to lay out the rhythm.

When I finished playing, he said, "Show Jack," so I started to show Jack DeJohnette. It was really just one of those simple rhythms, you know, but you had to have some kind of weird coordination to get it right. Jack couldn't get it, so Miles looked over at me and said, "Stay there." I sat behind the drum set on "Miles Runs the Voodoo Down," a tune on what became a gold album. Oh boy, oh boy! I was in seventh heaven, ladies and gentlemen. It was just so incredible.

After the "Bitches Brew" session, I continued touring and recording with Nina, and she put me on salary. At that time to be put on salary was considered a kind of feather in your cap because it meant that you still got paid even when you weren't working. Then it happened. I got the call to play with Miles Davis. Needless to say, all hell broke loose with Nina. Of course, all kinds of my feelings surfaced because I was extremely loyal to her and respected Nina for teaching me so much but then again, it was Miles Davis.

Nina called up Miles and cursed him out for stealing her drummer. I lost contact with her for quite some time because she wouldn't have anything to do with me. I'd been her musical director as well, but I think that deep down she understood why I went with Miles. She was mad though. Mad to the point that Miles would call me up and rasp, "Don, get that bitch off my back."

I went to Miles' first rehearsal with a drum set because I thought he had hired me to play drums after that "Bitches Brew" session. When I walked in lugging my drum set, Miles looked at me and said, "Don, what are you doing with that? I can't find anyone to play percussion like you, and I already got two drummers. I'm teaming you with another percussionist." It was Mtume, the nephew of the great sax player Jimmy Heath. The drummer was Leon Chancler, who had changed his name to Ndugu. Mtume and Ndugu started to hang out a lot together and for reasons I won't mention, the drums became a major problem. Ndugu had brought along a Tony William's kind of set, a really small eighteen-inch bass drum. Miles was into his Buddy Miles sound and was always complaining to Ndugu trying to get him to take the head off the bass drum and to take off his rings and watch. Ndugu's hair was braided and Miles would say, "Play like your braided hair," because back then if your hair was braided, you were supposedly really Black.

Mtume didn't draw from Afro-Cuban or Latin roots in percussion, though he had his own unique sound. Miles wanted both Mtume's sound and mine, so I tried to compliment Mtume's music with my Afro-Cuban roots. I played conga drums without any small percussion instruments aside from the occasional cowbell, and we were really trying to make our sounds merge. I really wanted it to work, but it was difficult to make the sounds compatible 'cause of the personal tension going on. If I mentioned that I was going to play three conga drums, he'd tell me that was what he was going to do. I'll skip any other details, but I can tell you it was a real drag.

Contrary to certain individual's belief, there are a lot of soulful people of many colors out there who can play percussion and drums. People of Africa and of African descent have that natural indigenous thing happening. But travel the world, and you'll find a lot of other people out there that can play our music.

Later on, Miles had Airto, a percussionist, along with Naná Vasconcelos, who was well-schooled in Brazilian hand percussion. They really changed the course of fusion by introducing new textures and sounds. On parts of "Live/Evil" Miles used Airto. I have to say that Airto was the one who showed hand drummers like me about the small hand percussion. I had really shied away from smaller percussion instruments for a long time 'cause I didn't want to deal with it, so it was a great investigation as a conga player.

What an amazing time we had being on tour with Miles. We traveled everywhere. We went to Paris to do a concert alongside Duke Ellington. The Duke was so innovative musically and was such an elegant and humble man, he even rode in the back of the plane with his musicians. After Paris, we went to Copenhagen. Michael Henderson and I started hanging out 'cause we both loved that quest of which one of us would get the most exotic women in different countries. Now that was a wonderful time.

One night, Michael and I were downstairs at the concert hall when we were summoned upstairs to Miles' dressing room. I walked in and there was this masculine looking, Black woman wearing a mannish suit semi-shouting in Miles' ear. She was saying things like, "I knew you when you were nothing. You weren't shit!" That was the caliber of invectives she was throwing out. Miles was very annoyed and turned around and said, "Don, get this bitch out of my dressing room." We were just about to perform, so Michael and I reneged. We played the concert and afterwards Michael picked up a beautiful woman. While we were all standing around talking, we were summoned again. We went upstairs and as Michael and I went into the dressing room, we heard the same woman cursing him out. Miles once again requested us to get her out. She was really annoying him. Michael wanted to leave right away and I just didn't want to get involved. As we turned to walk down the hallway, we heard a loud smack and then a thud. We knew immediately it was a body hitting the floor. We looked and saw Miles

31

pulling this woman by the hair down the hallway. Miles pushed the elevator button and threw her in. The girl with Michael was so shocked that she started screaming like a cartoon character and ran away. Through the open staircase we watched the elevator open onto the lobby floor and heard the screaming. Miles turned around to us and said, "No bitch is gonna talk to me like that." You make your own judgment there.

The sequel is that the next night we were in the Montmartre Club, a very famous jazz club in Copenhagen. The sax player, Brew Moore, a very fragile, elderly man, walked in and told us that it was his wife who Miles had knocked out. He challenged Miles to a fight, and Miles instantly accepted and escorted him outside. It couldn't have been any kind of contest since Miles was a boxer in his spare time and would have annihilated Brew Moore in a flash. I had to break up the fight. There was no way old Brew was going to win. End of story.

That week, Michael and I went into a sex shop where they sold all sorts of condoms with roosters and hands with contraptions on them. We happened to go to a live sex show later and the people were doing their thing, so of course, we went back and told Miles about it. He took the whole band to the sex show after our gig! Miles said in his inimitable raspy voice, "Don, ask the sex show if they want to come back to the hotel." I did! But they declined.

The next stop was La Scala in Venice. It was a six o'clock gig and Miles was nowhere to be found. The Italian audience was so angry that they were throwing toilet paper and screaming *buffone*, which means clown. Hours passed and still nobody knew where he was.

At nine, he sauntered in. Amidst all the noise, Miles put his horn to his lips, started to play and within two seconds the raucous crowd grew silent. At the end of the concert Miles received a standing ovation and he took a bow. It was the first time that Miles ever came out for a bow. Keith Jarrett and I were so overwhelmed that it brought us to tears.

We then went to Yugoslavia to play at a jazz festival with Thelonius Monk, Art Blakey and so many other greats. I happened to meet an American girl who was going to school in Yugoslavia, and we bought a bottle of something and went back to my room. We had a wonderful night, but then I got a telephone call around seven in the morning. It was Miles. "You want to wake up?" "Sure," I said. I didn't care who was in the room, you know, and when it came to Miles, privacy was not an issue. When Miles arrived, he reached into his trumpet and pulled out some yellow pills. He looked at me and said, "How you want to take it? You want to crush it up and snort it?" I said, "I'll take it the way you do." We snorted the pills, and they were uppers all right.

For five hours Miles sat in my room and ran the gamut on boxing, Charlie Parker, the groups with Philly Joe Jones and Red Garland, and how those guys were strung out. He told me he loved to watch the musical battle between Trane and Sonny Rollins on stage together. I had five hours of history that I could try to share with you, but let me just say that Miles told the stories better than I ever could.

Anyway, the girl was still in my room and she offered to take Miles around the city. I was proud to give the girl to Miles, and they both left. We met at the airport that evening and he walked over to me and said, "Don, I had a good time, man. And guess what? I didn't even fuck her." I guess that was his way of showing a little bit of respect, you know.

Another time Miles called me to play at the Newport Jazz Festival. The gig was fantastic as always, but afterwards I noticed that Miles had shorted me by twenty-five dollars. Normally, no one would bitch about the pay due to the fact that it was an honor just to be playing with him! Though Miles had always been fair with the money, I decided to make a point of it because of the principle of the matter. So I went over to him, and just as I brought up the subject, someone snapped a photograph of me whispering in his ear that you may, in fact, see someday. Miles turned to me and said, "You know, Don, I shouldn't pay you the twenty-five dollars because you never made the rehearsal." The funny thing was there were never any rehearsals. We both broke up laughing and I got my twenty-five.

Performing with Miles was exciting every time with all focus upon him, though I was the only percussionist he let solo. We had this one gig in Rochester, New York, that was particularly memorable. Miles had this drummer at the time who had previously played with a great funk band and had a terrific heroin problem. We were all waiting for him to show up for this gig. One hour passed, then two, and the audience was getting impatient. Everyone was telling me to get ready to go on as the drummer. I didn't want this guy to lose his job, yet I really wanted the chance to play drums. Then he strolled in. Miles gently asked in his gravelly voice, "How do you feel?" He was ok and we went on to play. The drummer sounded terrible, slowing down the tempo when it shouldn't have been. Miles had displayed this compassionate, patient side that not too many people had seen. I just think there were many misconceptions about Miles' personality. That gruff, outer persona gave way a lot to a much kinder man, or at least that's what I saw.

One morning we were all going to the airport in London. We were standing in the lobby when Miles said, "Don, come with me." It was not a secret that Miles was into drugs, but this is just to illustrate his capacity. We went to the home of a Japanese guy, who gave Miles a huge, glass tube about six inches long, and three-quarters full of coke. Miles snorted the whole thing on the way back to the airport. The amazing thing is that he fell asleep on the plane ride home. Now, we're talking tolerance.

Miles eventually decided to take about five months off to hang out at a villa somewhere. I think it was with Julia Greco at that time but I'm not sure. I had a family and two kids and couldn't afford any kind of break, so I took a job loading tires on a railroad. I was just throwing these car tires into a boxcar, and it was tedious and exhausting. One day the foreman came up to me and asked if I was a student. "No," I told him, "I'm a musician." "Oh," he said, "who do you play with?" When I told him I played with Miles Davis, he wanted to know what the hell I was doing on the railroad, and so did I! Even this White foreman knew who Miles Davis was.

Now you have to understand what it meant to play with Miles Davis. How many musicians have dreamed of playing with him but never got the chance? I got the chance. I got my golden opportunity.

If I never see another light of day, if I never hear another note or touch another drum, playing with Miles will remain one of the highlights of my career.

6.

Mongo Santamaria/Lou Rawls

Around 1971, I was still going back and forth from Providence to New York a couple of times a week. I got a call to possibly join Mongo Santamaria and Armando Peraza, more idols of mine. Mongo and Armando had been part of the Cuban congeros who came to the States along with players like Chano Pozo, Francisco Aguabella, and Julito Collazo. What amazing musicians. Story has it that Armando, orphaned at age seven, lived on the streets of Havana and survived by selling vegetables. Man, talk about coming a long way.

Well, I went to the audition and Mongo hired me. Mongo had Ray Maldonado on trumpet, Eddie "Gua Gua" Rivera playing bass and Neal Creque on keyboards. I'm a non-Latin cat but I had those rhythms down. Armando taught me the true meaning of that timbale

37

roll, which is often played at the beginning of some Latin tunes. Oh, did we have so much fun in that band! We had a circuit playing in Atlanta. We also played up in Boston, the place where I initially had my first musical experiences and here I was back, only this time playing with Mongo. Oh God, did I feel proud playing with those guys.

Anyway, I was in between gigs with Tony, Mongo and Elvin. Sometimes they would take vacation time and I really needed to make some long money, you know,so I went out with the great Lou Rawls. Now ladies and gentlemen, this was my first venture into Hollywood and Las Vegas. About that time I was really having problems with my marriage and I met someone on the road who I thought was the most beautiful girl in the world. I hate to say anything negative, but this girl's occupation was, shall we say, suspect. I fell in love with her because she was absolutely gorgeous and I wanted her off the street. I gave up my family for her and we moved in together.

I remember my first gig with Lou at Century Plaza in L.A. Oh man, the stars came out - people like Debbie Reynolds and Connie Stevens. I even wore a tuxedo. Imagine me playing in a tuxedo! Here I am out in Hollywood with Lou Rawls making good bread. Some of it was going to alimony, but hey, back in those days six hundred, seven hundred bucks a week was pretty good money. I ran into percussionist Walfredo de los Reyes who was working with Wayne Newton. He told me about a drummer/percussionist who was playing with a house band at the Desert Inn named Alex Acuna. We ended up jamming a lot together and he went on to play with a list that included Elvis Presley, Diana Ross, Ella Fitzgerald, Whitney Houston, Weather Report,

Chick Corea and so many others. Man, he's such an amazing talent.

It was always a hell of an experience though for me to play with Lou. He was a quintessential cabaret performer and I had fun meeting all the movie stars. Shirley MacLaine was playing over in the big room when we were working at MGM on Christmas. Since I was born on Christmas Day, I got dressed up really sharp. Somehow or other she found out that it was my birthday, and as I walked by her dressing room, she came out and man, she gave me the biggest kiss. Today, when I watch Shirley MacLaine on TV or see her in the movies, my lips still tingle.

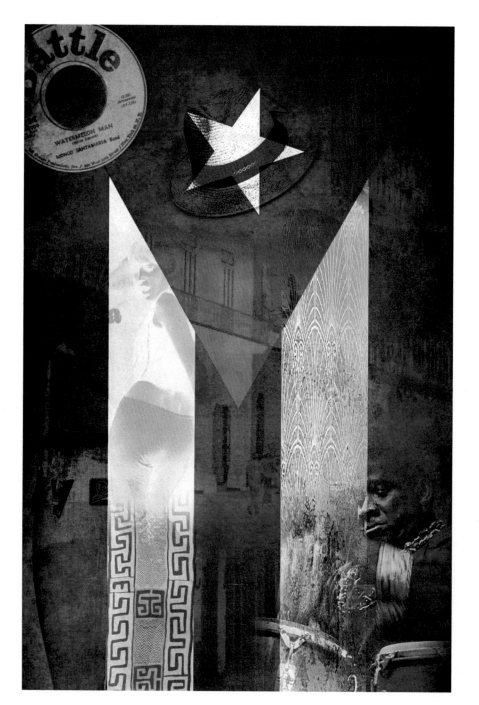

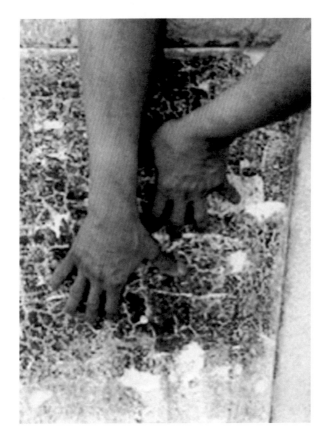

7.

Elvin Jones

Pretty soon, I got one of the most challenging gigs of my life.

Growing up there were two top groups in the jazz scene. There was Coltrane with McCoy Tyner, Elvin Jones and Jimmy Garrison, and then there was Miles Davis with Tony Williams, Herbie Hancock, Ron Carter and Wayne Shorter. Well, I landed a record date with Elvin Jones, who I considered to be the world's greatest contemporary jazz drummer. As a conga player and percussionist, working alongside with

Elvin Jones was on the same level as working with Miles Davis any day.

One night Elvin broke one of his tom toms. He turned to me and said, "Don, why don't you go over there and play the drums while I fix my toms." I mean, hey, to play behind Elvin Jones, I definitely wanted to take the challenge. I went and sat behind his drums and damn it, if we didn't play a really slow, slow ballad that needed brushes. At that time, the relationship between brushes and me was like oil and water, meaning I didn't have a clue what was happening. Man, my brushes got caught in the cracks of the drums. You could hear me stumbling. Master of brushes said, "Don, you know something? You're a non-brush playing mother fucker." No shit. I knew it was time to learn.

We did that record "Merry-Go-Round" and I think it was the first time Chick Corea recorded the tune "La Fiesta." After we finished the recording, I went out on the road with Elvin, Steve Grossman, Dave Liebman and Gene Perla. Grossman was coming onto the scene and had his own unique style since he'd been working with Miles. Liebman and my good buddy, Gene Perla, were getting their own sound too. Elvin didn't have a keyboard player, but every once in a while we'd play with Jan Hammer. Jan was a Czech prodigy who had attended Berklee College of Music, and there was no question about it that he was up and coming.

We'd all had an association from playing together in the New York City lofts. These lofts were basically the homes of musicians who opened their doors for jam sessions. It most certainly became a breeding ground for great music. Gene Perla and Jan Hammer lived together in this one loft by South Street near all the fish markets and I'd occasionally stay there just to play. We became a built-in rhythm section with drums, bass and piano, and every sax player wanted to jam with us. There was Bennie Maupin, Dave Liebman, Steve Grossman, Joe Farrell and so many others. Jan Hammer was really showing his incredible talent and we felt that he was the only player for Elvin's band. So we called Jan from the road to join us, but he chose Mahavishnu instead. Jan was really hooked on Mahavishnu and it was just more appealing to him.

By the way, when Mahavishnu had its first rehearsal, Billy Cobham couldn't make the gig and guess who filled in for him? That's right, your boy. Mahavishnu's music was fast and complex with those Indian influences. I only did one rehearsal, but that was all right because there was something very unnatural for me about playing in odd time signatures like 9/8. African rhythms followed your heartbeat in 4/4, 2/4 or at most 6/8. Man, if your heart ever went 9/8, you would be in big trouble. I think Mahavishnu wanted Gene Perla too, but Gene was so happy playing with Elvin that he didn't want to fool around with that signature stuff. He just wanted to swing out and get next to the right cymbal that Elvin was playing. Rick Laird took the bass part, and of course, Billy Cobham was the regular drummer with Jan Hammer on keyboards. The band had ego problems, but it was a great band and my first venture into serious fusion.

It was at a time when the big word "fusion" started to jump heavily into music. Elvin was playing straight-ahead jazz, and although Jan played a bit with us, he didn't stick around for too long. Who cared if it was straight ahead? Elvin showed me that he was the world's greatest drummer. He would play every time as though it were his last performance. He put himself into his music ferociously with all his polyrhythmic, dynamic phrasing. Man, at the end of the night, there was a pool of sweat underneath Elvin's snare drum and I had to dip my fingers in ice water. My hands pained me so much, I couldn't shake hands with anyone.

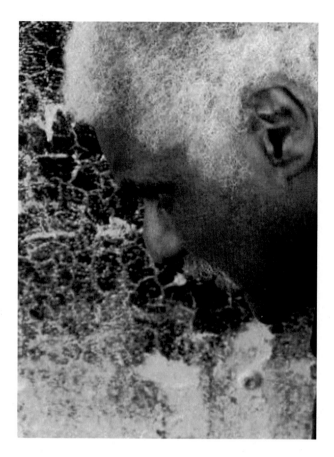

8.

Tony Williams

Tony Williams. What an amazing jazz drummer, man. He came along during the Miles era and was one of the musical revolutionaries from the time span that also included Ron Carter, Wayne Shorter and Herbie Hancock. Tony started out when he was just a kid but could hold his own with the greats. I was glad to see him breaking beyond straight-ahead drumming with avant-garde rhythms. He was always interested in Latin music even when we had that quartet up in Boston with Chick Corea on piano. Tony played drums and also palitos, which are sticks you often hit on a wooden surface. One day Tony called me up and said, "Man, bring your timbales over to the pad." I went over to where he was living just above Miles, and taught Tony the rhythm called Mozambique. It was a popular rhythm in New York at that time and it was Eddie Palmieri who was instrumental in bringing it around. Tony really wanted to learn it. If you listen to the record "Miles Smiles," you'll hear that rhythm and on "Footprints" too.

Tony decided to get a band together called Ego and we did a really great record with Ron Carter, Ted Dunbar and Warren Smith. Tony wanted to go out on the road you know, so he took those musicians plus Juini Booth, Larry Young (who had been working in "Lifetime"), and me. Warren, at the time, was one of the first young, Black, legitimate percussionists on the New York scene. By legitimate, I mean academically schooled in drums. Tony wrote the music for the band around the drums, so it was a really unique sound. I begged Tony to play that one tune called "Pee Wee" because I loved it so much.

At one point, while the band was on the road, Joe Chambers replaced Warren Smith on percussion. I tip my hat to Joe because he read that music like it was nothing, without hardly any practice. Man, what do you say when you're sitting alongside drummers like Elvin Jones and Tony Williams? What can you say

Once, when we were playing in a club in New York, Miles came by to see the band. Tony had gotten upset that night for some reason or another. The music just wasn't right and Tony stormed off

45

the bandstand. I remember Miles standing backstage. He then grabbed Tony, looked at him and said, "Tony, you can't force your music on anybody." I've always kept that in mind. Tony's music was really special and either you loved it or you didn't.

9.

Trini Lopez

I was sitting in my pad and work was really slow. It was 1974 in L.A. and a really bad time for a musician like me, owing alimony with no gigs in sight. There was just nothing to pay the upcoming bills, and then the phone rang. It was a musician acquaintance, and I say acquaintance because I forget his name. We carried on a casual conversation in which he knew that I had played with Miles Davis, Nina Simone, Chick Corea and others. After conversing for a while, he nonchalantly said, "I'm playing this gig at the Balboa Country Club and they need a percussion player, preferably congas and bongos. You've worked with so many famous musicians, I wouldn't dare ask you to do this gig." I asked in a voice with overtones of Mr. Hyde and then back to Dr. Jekyll, what to wear, what to bring and what it paid. On the other end of the phone this guy was whooping and hollering so I guess he was glad that I was doing it, and so was I.

The gig was with the high-profiled, talented Trini Lopez. Trini had gained recognition when "Lemon Tree" and "La Bamba" hit the charts and appeared in the very popular movie, "Dirty Dozen," which didn't hurt either. Mr. Lopez was in fact one of the "Dirty Dozen." That night I had a ball when I played congas. He gave me a little solo spot to stretch out on and I got paid five hundred smackeroos. Everything turned out all right, except I almost didn't make it to the gig.

On my way, I stopped at a gas station to find out where this Balboa Country Club was. It was in an area I didn't frequent – a rich area. There were two fairly young guys standing alongside the gas pump. One was in gas station attendant attire and the other in black leather gear, his fat butt perched on a fine motorcycle. He had his helmet tucked under his arm as he gave the attendant some dough. I got out of my car and walked toward them to ask if they knew where the country club was. There was no way I could have or would have thrown out any bad vibes. Before the gas station attendant could speak, this motorcycle dude uttered, "Sorry, I don't talk to Niggers." Yea, yea, yea, I'm thinking, here we go again. I grew up in an environment where anything derogatory said by a White person was an entry for them to kick your ass. The blood rose to my head, and I immediately planned what course of action I should take. I formulated running him over in my car. I got in my car and sat behind the wheel not thinking of any consequences, just the plain act of running this man over on his motorcycle. The gas station attendant was telling me, "Hey man, don't pay any attention to him," but by this time I was seeing purple. I sat there waiting for him to get back on his bike. He walked over to it and as he was putting his leg over, some divine message came to me. I thought, if I do this, I'll be locked up, and more importantly, not be able to get the money from the gig to pay child support. My career clearly would be ruined because I would have killed him. I sat there reasoning with myself and finally voted not to run him over. Even so, I still went back there every day for three days looking for the guy.

I found out that he was part of some Hell's Angels Motorcycle club. I still veer away from people who wear black leather and ride motorcycles. Although the gig with everyone dressed in their finery and me in a tux was great, that episode of racism still stuck with me.

10.

Blood, Sweat & Tears;

Remnants of a Super Band

BS&T was a phenomenal group consisting of Bobby Colomby (an original member), Dave Bargeron, David Clayton-Thomas, Bill Tillman, Tony Klatka, Ron McClure, Lew Soloff and Larry Willis, who was a great pianist and a really good friend of mine. I was with Miles at the Newport Jazz Festival and after playing, BS&T asked me to sit in with them. They had never played with percussion so I said my usual,

"Sure, why not?" After that they offered me the gig.

Around 1974 I started touring the world with them. They were riding on the laurels of "Spinning Wheel" and we were spinning the world over. Bobby Colomby, who was really the head of the group, owned the name of the band and I think that the rest of the original members had sold their shares to him. They had great success but the only serious problem in BS&T was David Clayton-Thomas. I had gotten good advice prior to joining to stay away from him because he had a certain kind of personality, or shall we say, disorder.

The night before Halloween we had just finished our gig. Let me just say I certainly wasn't used to the show business thing of running off the stage and running back on to obtain applause, you know? So at the end of the gig, I sort of sauntered off the stage. Apparently, David didn't like my sauntering so he started rushing me off the stage. I came back with a little defense because I won't take that kind of "rushing thing." I guess my little macho ego got involved. David definitely picked up on my attitude so there was a slight chill in the air. I didn't want to be pushed around by anybody, especially after playing with all those great cats like Miles, Elvin and Mongo. They certainly were not into milking the audience for applause, though they received plenty.

The next day, the band dressed up for Halloween along with the audience, which consisted of vampires, assorted witches and the like. Jaco, who had been playing with the band prior to his record release, came as a 1950s Sha Na Na type greaser. Tony Klatka put on makeup and false eyelashes. I sprinkled some sparkle on my arms and

51

wore a cut off T-shirt. My attire had absolutely nothing to do with femininity, not at all. During the gig, David Clayton-Thomas started to introduce the members of the band. He presented Tony Klatka as the "resident faggot." *En masse* the audience sighed with disdain. It was obviously an unnecessary comment. When it was my turn, David announced, "and here's our percussionist, Don Alias, the queen from Los Angeles." Well, my blood pressure rose on that statement. I grew up in Harlem, you understand, and people just do not make reference to anybody being homosexual. Not that I had anything against it, but in the hood that was not considered a joke.

So, Bobby Colomby was on drums and I was on percussion. We were playing the intro to "Lucretia MacEvil" when I stopped playing, got up, walked over to my roadie and asked for a hammer. Then, in front of 20,000 people, while David Clayton-Thomas was singing, I put the hammer to his temple and warned him, "If you ever insult me again, this hammer will be for you." Then I went back and sat down behind my congas.

I was told immediately afterwards that David Clayton-Thomas ran up to one of the cars about to leave the venue. In it were Dave Bargeron and the band leader Bobby Colomby. Bobby rolled down the window and David told him what had just happened. He then gave Colomby an ultimatum; "It's either Don Alias or me, you choose!" Colomby who was not a big fan of David's either said, "You know, Don's a great percussionist and they're very hard to replace." I thought that was really great, man!

In retrospect, I have to say I was wrong. I apologize for that move. It was terrible. It was uncalled for, even though the band members dug it. After that incident, the BS&T members started calling me Thor. I apologize to you, David, for being such an asshole but then again, so were you.

Well, we toured, man, and Larry Willis really started writing some excellent material for BS&T. Luckily everyone had their roots in jazz. Larry Willis and Tony Klatka began to write some music that was really geared to big band fusion. Real hip tunes. We recorded some LPs and Larry wrote a hell of a tune, and Mike Stern took great solos. This period was the tail end of a great era where I was venturing into rock and roll.

We were performing in Tokyo and nearby was an American Las Vegas Revue. One particular night, the band invited the dancers from the show. Japanese men preferred blonde American women so all the dancers had to wear blonde wigs. The Japanese men would sit in the audience with binoculars just to get a closer look at these long-legged American blondes. Anyway, some of the dancers came to the gig and we started to play. At the end of our last tune, somehow or another David invited them up on the bandstand. About twenty-five girls were dancing on the bandstand and oh, what a sight. They all came back into the dressing room, and without insulting women, it was like choosing in a meat market. We could be heard saying, "No, I'll take this one, you take that one." All of a sudden they started to choose us. It was like a shuttle service in the hotel that night. That was the nature of our life with BS&T on the road. Crazy, crazy times.

We finished Japan and went to New Zealand, which I fell in

love with. I had noticed that David, our lead singer was taking a lot of downers and it was the first time I ever saw anyone collapse on stage. He hit into this tune and all of a sudden it got really silent because our boy fell right out on stage. Luckily, that was towards the end of the BS&T tour.

Right after that incident I met a fabulous New Zealand girl and instantly fell in love. She decided to drive me to Christ Church, which is at the tip of New Zealand. Man, what a beautiful country, what a beautiful woman.

After a year with BS&T, the end of its existence was nearing. The band had internal problems, conflicts with management, and eventually the musicians didn't want to have anything to do with it. We all just wanted to concentrate on our music. Then up pops Stone Alliance.

11.

Stone Alliance

I have to give it to Gene Perla for having a great business head. Gene, Steve Grossman and I gathered at my mother's house and we decided to form a band called Stone Alliance. Stone Alliance was going to be a venture into rock-jazz. I wanted to play loud, I wanted to improvise, and if I swung, I wanted to swing hard. The band was strictly a trio, no chord instruments. Grossman had the melodies and I could write them too. I was always called Three-Fingered Brown because I could pentatonic you to death in D flat on the piano. I didn't have to worry about the chords because when we would hit those melodies, man, that shit would be jumping off the bandstand. Gene was taking care of the business and I was concentrating on the music.

It was the makings of a dynamite trio, only one problem – Steve was into the mind-altering drug scene. I'm sure you know that some of us in the music business had problems avoiding the temptation of heavy drugs. Who knew what was going through Charlie Parker's mind? He was such a genius. Maybe he just couldn't cope, but it made no sense to delve into the kind of hell that drugs brought along.

Anyway, Steve was down there in the drug scene, shall we say, when we landed a State Department tour of Brazil and some parts of South America. It was our fifteen-day tour, which stretched into six months. Oh boy, we got our first vision of Brazil when the plane flew right next to that statue of Jesus Christ with outstretched arms to the sky. We came way too close to that statue. Gene said the look of fear on my face was something that you could never, ever duplicate.

I remember landing in the airport and a tune by BS&T was playing. It was a tune that Larry Willis had written. As you know, I had just recently quit that band. To me that was more than coincidence. Then everything got started. The first thing we did was go into a local bar and have what they call a Batida de Limao, which is a really strong drink made with fermented sugar cane, water, and lime juice. We drank it and got on a bus, and all I can remember was being drunk as a mother fucker man, traveling on that bus. Soon enough we began to meet some of the great musicians who were living there. We ran into Victor Assis Brasil and Paulo Moura, who was a soprano saxophone player, like the Wayne Shorter of South America.

Just before Carnival, Paulo took us to an area called Manguere, which was known as the Samba School. You could hear the music bouncing off the hills up in the Favela, which is the slum area of Brazil. Man, I stood on the street and listened. It was like a wave overtook me and that Brazilian music started seeping into my bones. Thank you, Paulo Moura.

We hit during Carnival and the air was full of electricity. The music was in the streets with people dancing in the most colorful and outlandish costumes you can imagine. I'd gotten into playing a Bata drum, a religious drum, and white was one of the colors of the God, Obatala. Gene's mom had made white suits before we left so when we played man, we looked like rock musicians though both jazz and rock audiences loved us.

We traveled to Chile and stayed for about a month. Gene and I caught the Chilean Revenge and got terribly sick. Probably from brushing our teeth with the water, or something that had to do with organisms. I remember doing a television show then. Grossman was strung out and I got into a fistfight with him about it. I hit him in the mouth and he got an infection in his lip and I got an infection in my hand. Boy, we watched the video of that TV show with us sick and drugged and yet we still had a ball playing!

While we were traveling around South America, we went to Montevideo, Uruguay, which is the home of the Candomble. Man, the Candomble is a heavy rhythm even for a drummer. It's something you just can't describe. You have to listen to it. We used to meet with the local musicians who played on the crates or wooden boxes in the market place. I infused that Candomble into my body. I wish I'd had more time to learn about each of the rhythms but I did use a bit of the Candomble on a future recording that we did in Argentina.

We traveled to Asuncion in Paraguay, and of course brought our blotter paper full of acid with us. By this time it had gotten soaked with water and all the acid was on one end of the paper, so we were taking some really concentrated hits. Don't forget that we were sponsored by the U.S. State Department and tripping on acid wasn't necessarily their idea of the best role models. On one occasion, the U.S. diplomat in Asuncion called us to his office and boy, did we get a lecture on our behavior, especially Grossman's habits. For some reason or another, Gene didn't take a liking to this guy, so when it turned out that we had a couple of things stolen from our dressing room that night, he let this diplomat really have it. Gene told him that he was irresponsible and didn't have any business reprimanding us about our behavior since he couldn't even keep our stuff from being stolen. Grossman and I really went off on Gene. I don't know if it was the acid we were taking that made us all sensitive, or if it was because I was afraid this diplomat might cut our tour short, but I was so mad.

Then our next stop on tour was Buenos Aires, Argentina, where we stayed for an entire month. Man, they really treated us like rock stars. The press did a newsreel that was shown in the movie theaters with scenes of us getting off the plane, signing autographs, doing the whole bit. Buenos Aires had such a mixture of different races. Italians, Spaniards and Africans. Most definitely there were some of the most beautiful women I'd ever seen in my life. We were the American jazz-rock stars of the moment and because of that we could pick and choose from the array of gorgeous women. It was my first venture into an apartment where you could go for a couple of hours since most of the women lived with their parents. Needless to say, I was in and out of those apartments. While we were in Buenos Aires, a girl with long, black hair, whose perfume you could smell before she entered the room, came back stage. She wanted to see Grossman. As it turned out, Grossman had been in Buenos Aires with this woman and later married her. Her name was Graciela. As a matter of fact, the tune with the Candomble rhythm was called "Graciela."

Grossman was going in and out of his drug thing at that time too, so things got tough. Our last gig on the tour was at Ronnie Scott's in London during the end of 1976. We had two weeks opposite Stan Getz. Hey, he was a great saxophone player, but we had Steve Grossman. We were ready to set Ronnie Scott's ass on fire, man, ready to turn that place down. Grossman had first stopped in Belgium at a pharmacist's place I don't need to name because all the musicians from the 70's knew this guy. I had a romantic encounter with this pharmacist's daughter, but what's more relevant is that Grossman had gotten some morphine suppositories.

We were all waiting around Ronnie Scott's for Grossman to come, and when he finally called he just said, "I can't make the gig." Man, why don't you just bend us all over, stick a foot in our asses, shove a dagger in our hearts and kill us? We were a trio, saxophone, bass and drums. All of a sudden, a dark shroud came over us all and our musical relationship with Steve Grossman ended. Stone Alliance didn't end, but our association with one of the greatest saxophone players did. We were down and had no choice but to go back home.

When I got back to the States, it was such a culture shock. I couldn't seem to talk to anyone, especially women. I didn't know how to relate to people. I had gotten used to a warm and open society where you made eye contact with feeling. People in New York seemed cold and closed. In Latin America and Europe, even sales people were welcoming, but here they had an attitude. There was a harshness that you don't necessarily notice until you've been away. Man, it took me such a long time to get back into my life in New York.

ALLIANCE

Exclusively on
P.M. Records, Inc.

20 Martha Street
Woodcliff Lake, N.J.
07675 U.S.A.

STONE

Gene Perla-
Basses
Performed and
recorded with
Willie Bobo,
Woody Herman,
Nina Simone,
Sarah Vaughan,

Don Alias-
Percussion
Performed and
recorded with
Nina Simone,
Miles Davis,
Mongo Santa Maria,

Steve Grossman-
Saxophones
Performed and
recorded with Miles
Davis, and Elvin
Jones. His first
record, "Some

Stone Alliance is a
newly formed group
of three well-known
American musi-
cians dedicated to
the creative

12.

Roberta Flack; Soul Sister

When Roberta first came on the scene, I was working with Nina Simone. I have to say that Nina was a bit jealous of Roberta. Maybe jealous of her instant popularity and that voice of hers. They had similarities in that they both sang and accompanied themselves on the piano. Nina's material was soul wrenching and politically oriented. Roberta, on the other hand was a true purveyor of love songs. She could make you cry when she sang with that mellow, dulcet voice of hers. She really hit it big in the 1970s; her music stemming from gospel roots mixed with cool, pop, love songs.

After I had fulfilled my dream of playing with Miles, I never really set goals to perform with specific people during my career. I always wanted to see where the music would take me. I really admired

Roberta's strength as a singer and as a woman. What really got me was the way she was so down to earth about absolutely everything. She epitomized a Soul Sister, or whatever you want to call someone who was always genuine, and true to herself.

It happened that the Prince of Saudi Arabia was having a birthday party and it was customary to invite musical guests to perform at his house. This time he invited Roberta to perform. One highlight of this event was getting to play drums with Richard Patterson on bass and Bernard Wright on piano. It sounded so good. Richard was the last bass player for Miles Davis and currently plays with David Sanborn. Bernard had been a child prodigy and played with the jazz giants. Here were musicians who truly had the whole spectrum of contemporary music together.

The band drove to Langley, Virginia, well known as the home of the CIA. Our car stopped at the base of a hill where perched above sat a mansion. What fascinated me most was their elaborate security system. Half a dozen well-conditioned men awaited us with bulging suit jackets intended to conceal their AK-47 machine guns. In front of our vehicle lay a hidden metal plate approximately three by seven feet. By releasing some switch, this plate was propelled out of the ground and blocked our car from advancing. Men surrounded us with metal detectors that screened our limousine from top to bottom. Further on were a number of men casually milling about but watching our every move. It was the Navy SEALS that we didn't see stationed up in the surrounding hillsides who were scrutinizing us. Talk about security.

The festivities of the evening had begun and the guests at this soiree were great political and governmental dignitaries, one of which was the Secretary of State. We were escorted to the prince's study, decorated with photos of himself in full regalia alongside air force jets that he had piloted. Quite impressive. While we performed, the prince, a good looking man in his forties, got up and danced pop style with his beauteous wife. Some of the two hundred dignitaries joined in and made sure to clap afterwards.

Another gig that stands out in my mind was Charlie Sheen's wedding. Charlie, a fine actor with a colorful life, was famous because of his movie career but infamous for his recent sexual escapades. It had to do with a woman and his chemical abuse but no need to elaborate. That story was already all over the tabloids and naturally had peaked my curiosity. I was eager to see which stars would be attending, and I wasn't disappointed. I'd always been such a movie buff that I recognized most of the prominent actors and actresses who were there. Ally Sheedy, Emilio Estevez, Rob Lowe, Robert Downey, Jr., etc. But for me the highlight was seeing Charlie's father, Martin Sheen. He's the one actor I extremely admired and respected. The movie, "Sugarland Express" with Goldie Hawn, was a classic, as well as "Apocalypse Now," but this isn't TV guide. Martin was kind and a little drunk, too.

Charlie Sheen loved Roberta Flack and wanted her love songs dedicated to his wife. Their favorite request was "The First Time Ever I Saw Your Face." The marriage only lasted six months but at that moment, bliss flooded the room. I guess you could attribute it to the champagne, which I was drinking too. Charlie ended up sitting by the side of the bandstand in an informal meet and greet situation. People were coming up to say hello and chat. Then it became the band's turn to greet Charlie. We all went over to him, and one by one shook his hand. When it came my turn, and, readers, up until this day, I can't figure out what the primary motivation for this gesture was, I reached out, tussled Charlie Sheen's hair as if he were a child of mine and gave some banal, generic greeting such as "congratulations, man!" Everyone shook Charlie Sheen's hand and I ruffled his hair. He looked up and smiled. Go figure. Again, another memorable result of playing music. I thank Roberta for all these incredible gigs.

Beyond any of these stories, I will never forget the day I had to tell Roberta that Miles had died. Man, it was a really tough time for us all. I was rehearsing at SIR studios with the amazing Marcus Miller, who had also played with Miles for quite a while. I hadn't seen Roberta in some time but she happened to be rehearsing in the next room. One of the guys at SIR had just heard over the radio that Miles had died, so when I stepped into the hallway on a break, he told me. It was really a shock and I had to take a moment to absorb it all.

I was standing around with the drummer, Steve Jordan, who at that time was rehearsing with Keith Richards of the Rolling Stones. It was obvious by the way Roberta was singing that she hadn't heard the news yet. For some reason or another I just decided to take it upon myself to tell her. You have to consider that she and Miles were really close, really tight. When Roberta walked out into that hallway, she was wearing that big, beautiful smile of hers which made it even more difficult for me to tell her. She was happy to see me after so long and I didn't want to bring her down. When we hit a lull in the conversation, I knew it was time for me to come out and just tell her that Miles was gone. She let out a tremendous wail, a tremendous scream. It was enough to make you break down. She ran to the telephone to call Finny, Miles' valet and companion. Finny was the one who did everyone's hair on the road. He was the one who gave us those big Jimi Hendrix Afros and also took care of Miles. Roberta called to ask Finny if it was true and he told her it was. We had to escort her outside and put her in a taxicab. Man, it was a rough day, a rough day.

13.

Joni Mitchell

Joni and I were living together working on our romance. She had found this amazing loft downtown on Varick Street for us. It was as large as a basketball court with a rooftop that overlooked the city. Just a wonderful place to set up shop to be creative. She was a prolific genius, a woman who wrote about what happened in her life. She was beautiful and sometimes so consuming. Because Joni was a household name at times it was difficult to maintain my identity, though I did have my own artistic life. Joni introduced me to all the heavies in Hollywood such as Jackson Brown, the Eagles, Warren Beatty and Bianca Jagger. I was Joni's mystery man to most of them and for all they knew, I could have been her pimp. Jack Nicholson though, who was going with Angelica Huston at that time, always made me feel welcome. He'd ask me, "What's in the can? You got anything in the can?" He knew what I was doing unlike the many I encountered. Thanks, Jack.

You have to keep in mind that I was a Black jazz musician hanging out with a White folk musician. Often, I didn't get a certain respect from the movie or high rock culture such as Crosby and Stills, though Nash and Young were gentlemen. Regardless of what anyone was thinking, Joni and I were enjoying each other's company and going through the normal ups and downs. At some point I'd taken Joni to New York City and introduced her to its jazz scene. She had a special depth that absorbed different cultures so I showed her my musical world with all the congeros and Afro-Cuban musicians.

One afternoon, Joni got a call from Charlie Mingus, who originally wanted her to recite T. S. Eliot over his music. Joni had gotten into jazz when she started working with drummer Johnny Guerin and since she was so open musically, it came naturally to her. I must admit that when she got the call from Charlie, she didn't know if he was interested in her famous name just to sell records, or her work. As soon as Joni hung up we got our excited asses in gear, jumped into a taxi and headed for Charlie's apartment. Sue Mingus answered the door and introduced us to Charlie. He was in the last throes of Lou Gehrig's disease, in a wheelchair, and was finding it increasingly difficult to swallow and talk. Somehow he managed to tell us of some wonderful episodes in his life. I remember Charlie showing us one of his old basses and all I could do was envision him playing his ass off with Charlie Parker. Charlie and Joni talked about poetry and it was decided that evening that Joni would write lyrics to his music. Man, what an honor!

Writing those lyrics set off a creative process in Joni that was like a hurricane. When she was involved in that process it was like another force took over and she'd be up at all hours pacing, smoking packs of cigarettes, creating. All of this could have been extremely intimidating for someone who didn't have himself together, but thank God, in most ways I did. I certainly won't pat myself on the back because there were those moments when I didn't handle some of the emotional situations in the best way. Joni was a sensitive, musical storyteller, and Charlie was an improvising be-bop player with a wry, sardonic sense of humor that you could literally hear in his music. This project would be the perfect marriage of folk and jazz.

We set up shop in the studio where Charlie began to tell us intriguing stories about his music. He told us that Lester Young in his pork pie hat had inspired the "Pork Pie Hat" tune. A pork pie hat was a jazz hat with a flat top and wide brim, which had became Lester Young's signature style. One afternoon, Mingus told us the story about Lester Young's parents, who were a bi-racial couple and both hoofers. When they used to travel around the Chitlin' Circuit down South they were confronted by a great deal of racism. The inspiration for the lyrics came to Joni one day when we were staying at The Park Hotel as our loft was being renovated. We decided to hit the town that night and so we took the train uptown getting off around 50th Street on the West Side. A few blocks from the subway we saw an awning jutting over a bar that said, "Pork Pie Hat Bar." I looked at Joni and she looked at me. It was like magic. We went into the Pork Pie Hat Bar, where there was a whole bunch of guys flamboyantly dressed playing backgammon. At the bar we ordered a drink just trying to soak it all in. Someone had selected a tune by Miles on the jukebox. I think it was "In Your Own Sweet Way" and a guy started tap dancing in front of the jukebox. We stood there for a while and I could just see those wheels churning in Joni's eyes. The tap dancer reminded her of the Chitlin' Circuit story Charlie Mingus had just told us.

By the time we had decided to split, a crowd had gathered outside. In the middle were two little Black boys on the sidewalk, damn cute kids, and guess what they were doing? They were tap dancing and people were throwing them money. We looked down the street and there was a restaurant, or maybe it was a grocery store, called Charlie's Place. When you listen to Joni's lyrics on that tune, you'll hear the story of Lester Young's parents. Like I said, it was magic, man.

Now the other kind of magic had to take place. We had to get the right rhythm section that would blend together to satisfy both Charlie and Joni. Stanley Clark came down to audition and we even had a session with John McLaughlin. I always tried to stay in the background, but one time they invited Gerry Mulligan to do some of the pre-session work and I knew I could swing. I at least wanted to let Charlie Mingus know that if he needed a real drummer, I could hook him up. And so it happened. What a thrill it was to sit in front of him and swing, and some of what we played became a prelude on the record. Joni recorded with contemporary jazz musicians like Jaco Pastorius, Wayne Shorter and Herbie Hancock, who was also a great friend of hers. At first there was something about Jaco's playing that Charlie just didn't like. Maybe he wanted an upright bass, maybe he wasn't too keen on Fender bass, but hey, we all knew that Jaco could handle the situation.

Not long afterwards, Mingus died in Mexico at age fifty-six before the project was finished. On the Mexican sands that day lay fifty-six beached whales. As he had requested, his family scattered his ashes in India.

Joni took the initiative and finished the project. She started thinking about going on the road again and, of course, I was in her band, no question. We had a stellar lineup with Jaco Pastorius, Pat Metheny, Lyle Mays and an acapella group called The Persuasions. They were a bad ass group, man who could sing you underneath the table. Jaco was the designated musical director, but didn't have much time to look for a drummer since he was in the midst of his thing with Weather Report. I found out later that he didn't really want to use a big band with Joni anyway. He wanted to go out with something small with Pat Metheny, Herbie Hancock, me, and maybe Alex Acuna from Weather Report, too. Joni had decided she wanted Mike Brecker along with Pat Metheny and Lyle Mays, but Jaco wasn't too keen on getting

70

them since he still envisioned that small group. Joni sometimes used great drummer, Peter Erskine, who later joined Weather Report after Alex and Manolo Badrena split. Unfortunately, Peter couldn't make Joni's gig, so we had to try out other drummers. No one really worked, so I decided that I wanted the drum chair. Man, I really wanted that gig. I couldn't see myself playing percussion next to any drummer who didn't know how to swing or especially who wasn't sensitive enough to play brushes on the ballads. Elvin Jones had taught me the finer points of playing brushes, which I would apply, so I vibed for the drum chair. I wasn't a heavy rock drummer, but if we were going in between rock and jazz, I could really hit.

It turned out that some people in the band weren't too happy about me playing drums. I think Pat Metheny would have preferred that I played percussion, not a regular drum set. I won't lie. I did my fair share of stumbling here and there, but I'm really proud of our gigs, especially the one at Santa Barbara, which we captured on video. Anyway, two weeks later, Jaco finally arrived after the rehearsals and all he could say was that he didn't know if he wanted Mike Brecker in the band. There was a bit of controversy about this and Joni had to sit us all down to work through everything. She really had an ability to spank Jaco, and man, she spanked him. I tip my hat to Mike Brecker because he wouldn't accept any of Jaco's wild nonsense. Mike would just tell him, "Hey man, what's with you? We haven't even played together, why don't you give me a chance?" Needless to say, after Jaco heard Mike, he couldn't do without him.

Anyone who was around at the time and saw Joni's band would

71

understand when I tell you it was a super, great band. A couple of those concerts were amazing. Her deep folk fans weren't always hip to her new sound, but they came out to the concerts anyway and ended up loving it.

Around that time, I got a call from a good friend of mine, Walfredo de los Reyes, Jr. to play percussion for Lola Falana. Walfredo was her drummer. Oh boy, Lola Falana, what a fine looking Black woman. She had made her claim to fame appearing in Golden Boy with Sammy Davis, Jr. on Broadway. Well, Lola and I really hit it off and we definitely had a little spark. Before we took off to Vegas, we taped The Johnny Carson Show. I got all shined up in a black, silk tuxedo and sat in front of Doc Severinsen's band. For some reason or another, Johnny took a liking to my conga playing and he was bangin' on his table like it was a conga all during the commercials.

When Lola came out on the stage, she was looking beauteous, man. When the show aired a few nights later, Joni was watching it with her cousin who said something like, "Are you going to leave him in Vegas with HER?" As it turned out, that night I did get a flirt from Lola. She invited me to a party with her but I declined because I was so ensconced in my relationship with Joni. I guess Lola thought it was unusual for any man to refuse a date with her. Lo and behold, the next morning, I heard a knock on the door from none other than Ms. Mitchell. I remember her saying with that warm smile of hers, "Ah, I think I'll spend some time with you here in Vegas."

Later that day, she went downstairs to play the slot machine and met a man who was actually a cleaner from Des Moines.

72

If you know Joni's music, she's singing the whole story for you in "The Cleaner from Des Moines." Listen to those lyrics, man. It all happened.

She caused quite a stir when I took her down to the show in Vegas that night, being the famous woman that she is. We went back out on tour soon afterwards with Joni's band and man, I'm telling you, when we played at Forest Hills in New York, everyone showed up. I invited my beautiful grandmother and family to come. They all loved Joni and I really loved Joni. Being romantically involved with the leader of the band made things difficult at times and we continued to have our ups and downs. She was an amazing woman though and not just because she was a great songwriter. That woman could paint her ass off too. She was a good friend and fan of Georgia O'Keeffe, so one afternoon, while Joni was visiting me in Vegas, we rented an RV and drove down to see her in Abiquiu, New Mexico.

Look at Georgia's painting and you can see all the eroticism you want to see in those flowers. She was a lovely woman who inspired me to write "Georgia O."

We continued touring with Joni's band and I have to say that the band got to where we actually liked each other. After a series of great concerts in the Midwest, we all got paid and I had a handful of hundred dollar bills. Joni and I decided to go shopping in an area of unapparent racial disharmony. We went into a department store looking for pants and cotton shirts. At the shirt department we paid with a hundred dollar bill and likewise when we bought the pants in another department. Our hundred dollar bills were being sprinkled all throughout the registers in that store. Upon leaving the store, I noticed a squad car rapidly pulling up in front. Three officers got out and were now walking towards Joni and me a bit too quickly for our comfort. "Hold it right there!" they shouted and demanded to know where we were going. I was caught by surprise and could only utter, "What?" They told us to go back into the store and had us stand with our faces towards the wall. They frisked and searched me, eventually pulling out my wallet with the remaining hundred dollar bills. One cop mockingly said, "Oh, look, he's got plenty of money." Then it dawned on me that this asshole had probably received a call from the department store that a BLACK man and a WHITE woman were throwing money around in their store.

They questioned us in a degrading manner, one saying, "Look at him, look at him, Mr. Big Shot." We felt totally disrespected by these White, Midwestern cops. Then a young clerk came running over shouting, "Do you know who that is?" Of course they looked perplexed, because they didn't. She yelled out, "That's Joni Mitchell!" Her co-workers turned around looking shocked and embarrassed as if to say, "You stupid mother fuckers." All of a sudden it became clear that they had made a huge error, and the cops sheepishly looked down at their shoes. Annoyed, Joni said, "We just got paid, we were only going shopping." They gave me back my money. Some of the clerks who had now formed a crowd were apologizing. "We're so sorry, Ms. Mitchell," some said, though the police never showed regret. This is one of the many experiences I've unfortunately had being on the road in America.

After the tour, Joni and I went back to our loft in New York just trying to make it together. Like I said, we had problems. Joni went to Los Angeles during that period of time and I think she fell in love with someone else. I had sensed something was wrong, so I strayed a bit too. I think the straw that broke the camel's back occurred when Joni was invited to Toronto to do a movie. I flew up to spend some time with her while she was working trying to keep things together (the movie was directed by a great Swedish actress). Joni was consumed with that movie and expected me to be as well. I was as supportive as I possibly could be, but I just couldn't be a "Mr. Mitchell" and besides my heart was with Stone Alliance back in New York City. I simply had other things I had to do.

After the third day, I split. I just walked up to her and said I couldn't stand being totally absorbed all the time with only her projects, and left. I think she needed more support from me, and by leaving I really put the period at the end of our sentence.

14.

Jaco Pastorius

I'd been touring supper clubs, posh hotels and concert halls with Lou Rawls for three years and now we had an engagement to do a television show in Miami. On the bill were also Morey Amsterdam and a female jazz singer. The rehearsal was at the luxurious Fontainebleau Hotel with gaudy chandeliers and red carpeting. When I walked into rehearsal, The Peter Graves Band, which was to be the backup band for the television show, was playing. I can tell you that the only sound I heard coming off the bandstand was the bass and it was something I had never heard before. I looked up and there was this gawky, lanky looking guy who was all ears. I think the words I said were, "Who are you?" He replied that his name was Jaco Pastorius. I introduced myself and apparently he knew who I was from all those Miles Davis records like "Bitches Brew" and "On the Corner."

From hearing Jaco play I knew right away there was something so unique that his sound had to become worldwide. We struck up a friendship like two high school kids. That night he took me to a club where the great multi-instrumentalist, Ira Sullivan was appearing and Jaco was playing upright bass with the band. There was also Alex Darqui and Bobby Economou, who later made Jaco's first record. We went on to have a very special creative partnership writing and continually playing together.

I remember the first time I played "Donna Lee" with Jaco. I didn't give it any thought to how unusual it was for a bass player to be playing that melody, let alone be accompanied by conga drums. It later became the signature tune for most aspiring bass players. Jaco, for a young musician, had this God-given talent how to play all of the old be-bop tunes and he could write his ass off. There's no question that he should be revered in the annals of influential musicians of the 20th century.

It was the 1980s and there had been quite a bit of substance abuse during the last decade. Though I don't want to dwell on the drug subject, just let it be known that it was prevalent. The following story was a result of abuse. It was not Jaco's normal state, which was really creative, loving and more sane than not. Jaco had left Weather Report and had already done a series of tours with bands that had a constant change of personnel. One particular band consisted of Mike Stern, Delmar Brown, Randy Brecker, Bob Mintzer, Othello Molineaux, Kenwood Dennard and myself. The musicians were fiery, intense. It was musical pyrotechnics. Audiences were primed to hear Jaco, especially after his brilliant stint with Weather Report. We had toured Japan, some of the East Coast in the States and now we were appearing in California at the Playboy Jazz Festival at the Hollywood Bowl.

Many people in the industry were anticipating this concert with Jaco, who would be sharing the bill with respected artists such as Tito Puente and Ella Fitzgerald. Sad to say, also at this time, Jaco was starting to experience bouts of manic depression. Before our tour to Japan, I received a call from American Airlines in Las Vegas. Jaco had attempted to board a flight without a ticket just proclaiming that he was the greatest bass player on Earth. Somehow he had thought that was enough to get him on board. While speaking with these authorities, I could hear Jaco's voice in the background shouting, "Don, Don, tell them who I am." Obviously he was already showing signs of instability. Up to this day, I had no idea how he got on the flight.

When we met in the airport for our Japanese tour, Jaco had shown up in a dress, though perhaps today that wouldn't seem so out of the ordinary. Take into consideration any outrageous thing that Jaco did was fine with the Japanese. No matter how bizarre he looked, they still accepted him. Keeping Jaco's steady decline in mind, we were now all heading to the Playboy Festival. Bill Cosby was the figurehead of this Playboy Jazz Festival as Quincy Jones was to Montreux. Bill Cosby had summoned me three days prior to the performance to give a tribute for Willie Bobo. It was an honor to have been asked by Bill, as Willie Bobo was the premier percussionist while I was growing up. Ironically enough, Jaco had played with Willie Bobo and Alex Acuna.

During those three days before Jaco arrived, the word was out about his behavior. It had been rumored that he'd been acting in bizarre ways and everyone was a little bit nervous about his arrival. Bill Cosby inquired about Jaco, but I couldn't divulge his personal problems. I thought that once Jaco had his bass in hand, no matter what his condition was he'd play his behind off. So far this had been consistently the case as it was in Japan. There he still played magnificently. I replied to Bill that I didn't know.

The day of the concert, Jaco arrived for the sound check at ten in the morning. He'd been up for three days, and quite obviously under the influence. The sound check consisted mainly of the band playing and Jaco running around the Hollywood Bowl end to end, supposedly listening. Jaco was in rare form, out of his fucking brains like I'd never seen before. First Jaco was throwing beer bottles around the dressing room. We were trying desperately to shield Bill Cosby from the events that were transpiring downstairs and we were running around trying to keep the doors closed. That night, Tito Puente and the members of his band were also in the dressing rooms. In the midst of Jaco's favorite phrase of "Who loves you?" he insulted Tito Puente calling him a *maricon*. TABOO!!!!!!!!!!! A no-no. This was the utmost in disrespect to this Latin icon. The members of our band had to do everything to hold back the members of Puente's band and entourage from crucifying Jaco. Through the grace of God, but especially Puente, everyone realized that Jaco was drunk and out of his mind. Puente showed great class and grace that night. While Tito was performing, Jaco ran on stage with no shirt interrupting his concert.

Now that the audience had gotten a glimpse of his strange state, the only thing that would save him would be a stellar, outstanding performance. Behold the moment of truth, as our band set up on stage behind our respective instruments. Before a note was played, Jaco (who now was in football makeup with black patches under his eyes and still bare-chested), came over to me and said, "Don, take a solo." This was the most inappropriate time to take a conga drum solo. That solo should have come in the middle of the show as planned. Everyone was completely flabbergasted, especially me. Knowing his mental state, I accepted the challenge and started to play.

About one quarter into playing, it really hit me how absurd this was to continue and so I slowly exited out of the solo. As soon as I did that, Jaco ran over to Kenwood and hollered at him to take a drum solo. Kenwood immediately started beatin' on those drums. Now, Kenwood is one dynamic and explosive drummer. So, it's not to say that he didn't sound amazing, but the music was getting chaotic. In the midst of this cacophony, I got up to reach for a hand percussion instrument. When I turned around, Coke Escovedo was blindly beating on my congas. Apparently, Jaco, in his burnt out state, had asked Coke to sit in. Not to take away from his expertise, but Coke had no business sitting behind my congas. Then I heard the sound of a trumpet. It was not Randy Brecker's sound but of that fine trumpeter, Johnny Coles. Without informing the band, Jaco had asked him to sit in. Once again, it was not the right thing to do. Hold on, the best is yet to come.

Jaco turned up his bass to full volume and threw it across the stage. When it hit, it sounded like a 747 had landed in the Hollywood Bowl, or use your imagination for the most thunderous sound there could be. It was the ultimate sonic boom. Under different circumstances this may have been a great opening for a Lollapalooza concert, but for the Playboy Jazz Festival this was beyond inappropriate. It was the first time that I had ever performed with Jaco Pastorius where he was jeered, whistled and booed. My heart sank and I bet the musicians who were backstage watching felt the same way. The "piece de resistance" was that Bill Cosby, observing all this fiasco shouted out, "TURN THAT STAGE AROUND!" The stage revolved, the lights went down and it was over.

At that moment it was clear that Jaco was on a death wish and I could not stay around to see it or help him. No one could help him and that night I quit the band. I don't think about his death because I am in denial. When I do, I realize we have again lost one of the great ones, and I have lost a great friend.

15.

The Girl Next Door;

Beauty is in the Behind of the Holder

In the interim of all these amazing musical experiences, I'd gotten married again and once more a divorce was in progress. My soon to be ex-wife, was a lovely, artistic woman, but unfortunately things don't always work out the way you hoped they would. It had been an extremely stressful separation and by no means was I looking for a mate. I'd now given up on relationships, especially permanent ones. I was resigned to not wanting any responsibilities in that area as the ending of the relationship had left deep emotional scars.

Then one day, I encountered a guy in the elevator in my building. He had this long, guitar player hair. I struck up a general conversation and found out that he was the brother of the woman who had just moved in next door to me. My curiosity was peaked and a few days later, I had a chance to meet my new neighbor. Let me state again that it could have been Sharon Stone or any other beauty next door and I would not have been interested.

Prior to our meeting, I heard muffled conversations through a wall we shared. You could hear voices quite well and even more with the use of such an amateur device such as a glass. I bring this bit of information up only to say that sometime in the future, one of us, because of the close proximity of the beds on the other side of the wall, became privy to sounds of a somewhat amorous nature. Not a good thing from one or the other's perspective. You DIG!!! Use your imagination.

Anyway, getting back, I knocked on the door and a very attractive woman with silver hair answered. I would guess she was in her late fifties or early sixties. Right away I thought, a little too old for me. I introduced myself with banal pleasantries of welcome to the neighborhood etc., etc. Right away she informed me that it was her daughter who was moving in, not she. This gave me feelings of a bit of fear, and of course, more curiosity. Fear because this woman was attractive and I envisioned her daughter to be this complete irresistible beauty. We chatted amicably for a bit and said goodbye.

Several days later, my doorbell rang and when I opened it, the fear factor reared itself again. My neighbor, Mel, was an extremely beautiful and interesting creature. She flashed her great smile and her blue eyes made my heart dance. She introduced herself and started to talk about our mutual musician friends. The charm came out of this woman like an exploding waterfall. I knew immediately that we were going to be close, though I didn't know in what capacity.

In the following weeks, we started to talk at each other's doorways. The conversations became longer and more interesting. Listen, she was next door, you dig? I thought if we hooked up people would say, "how convenient." Oh, she really peaked my curiosity all right. I wanted to show her that I genuinely liked her so I would buy her a newspaper and slide it under her door. What was so different about this gesture is that I had absolutely no ulterior motives. I liked her. I really, really liked her.

Now as it turned out, by nature I am an extremely private person. I am self-entertaining and thoroughly enjoy visual entertainment, so television was a partial companion for me. I am not one to invite friends to my apartment to hang out and party. Consequently, my behavior peaked her curiosity. She wondered because occasionally she'd ring my doorbell and I'd answer with all the lights off in the middle of the day. I'd stand stretching my T-shirt over my private parts while trying to hide behind the door. Couple this with the fact that she'd catch me coming home with videos from Blockbuster, leading her to speculate that I stayed home all day watching pornos or engaging in some kind of perversion. Of course, none of the above was true though her deductions were understandable.

We got closer and closer and it grew to light kisses on the cheek. I must mention that amongst her creative endeavors – painting, singing, writing, video, she was a professional dancer with a beautiful dancer's body. She had these gorgeous, shapely legs and possessed the ass of doom. As I always say, beauty is in the behind of the holder.

In the following months we became real tight. My instincts told me "no, no, no don't do this." I tried pushing her away and we went through the go away, come here, go away syndrome that couples can go through. In the interim, I had been corresponding with and occasionally seeing a number of women. I even went so far as to set Mel up on a blind date with a friend of mine.

I was playing at Birdland one night and invited Mel down to hear me perform. As well, I invited this musician friend of mine, Mark. Hell of a vibe player, I must say. Everything was going well until I glanced over and saw him reach down and squeeze Mel's leg. I found out later that he was supposedly "testing the dancer's calf." Sure, right. I became instantly jealous and he instantly became my far away, no communication, no seeing acquaintance. Although, in the beginning I was trying to set them up, in the end, I insisted she take the cab back to the apartment complex with me. I felt protective and the actual proprietor of her. No one, and I mean no one, was going to touch her.

We communicated in the coming months with letters under the door and then I made a serious mistake. I invited a Japanese girl I was in contact with to visit me from Tokyo. Rather than go into detail about the encounter, I'll go back to those thin walls between us. I duly emphasize the word thin. The head of my bed was literally on the other side of her bed. A definite no-no boys and girls, especially boys. Truly not a good way to establish a new relationship. I tried to renege on the invitation, but the young woman had already bought her ticket. Now no matter how I go on record saying what moans and groans that were heard, certain things were not consummated. I guess that's like saying I didn't inhale. Well, again, I will trust my reader's imagination.

During this time, I also decided that I didn't want to die alone and that I had better act upon this and choose a mate. I was getting a bit tired of my solitude. So, I asked my dear, old mother, since mothers know best about women. I called Mom up and gave her all the pros and cons about the girls I had chosen. I must admit that I was truly partial and favored my neighbor, Mel. My mother told me to give her some time to think about it and she would call me back.

I must say that the end decision was definitely mine, but I really wanted to hear what she had to say. She called me up about two hours later and gave me her opinion on the list of women I'd selected. My mother chose Mel, whom she had met prior to this. Now my mother only cared for a small number of women that I was involved with. Fortunately, she took to Mel like bees to honey, just like me.

The closer Mel and I got with each other, the more confused I became. At times I'd just push her away. Then we'd argue, make-up, argue and make-up some more. One sign of making up was that she'd put my favorite candy in front of my door. It was our sign of truce. But when I pushed her away once too often, I received a letter under my door saying that she'd completely given up on me.

One night, I could have sworn she had male company at her apartment. That next morning, I knocked on her door. I offered her my car service to drive her to work even though I knew she rode her bike every day. Actually, it was just my excuse to get into her apartment and check it out. Maybe it was my emotions affecting my hearing. She let me in, refused the ride and went to work. No one was there. Then, of course, after my panic, I subsequently pledged my undying love for her.

At this moment as these words are being written, we're still together and without the risk of sounding overbearing, I'm over the top in love. In admiration and respect for my neighbor I will say that I've waited such a long time to meet and fall in love with a beautiful person you can call your soul mate. When I squeeze her hand, when I watch her sleep, I know she's the one. I want to bring her around the world and tell everyone, "Hey, this is my girl, Mel."

16.

Chuck Mangione

I was touring a lot with Chuck both nationally and internationally. One day we'd be in Santo Domingo and another in Las Vegas. I decided to take my girl with me whenever I could, and this time we were going to Korea. We arrived in Seoul on a weekend and boy, those streets were lit up like Times Square. Hoards of people were stumbling drunk, real loud, real happy. We stopped at food carts, and 'cause I can eat just about anything, I ended up with a battered, boiled egg on a stick looking like a strange popsicle. Hey, when in Korea…

Chuck was still playing to sold-out audiences enthusiastic with his classic tunes like "Bella Via," "Chase the Clouds Away," "The Children of Sanchez" and so many others. Chazz Frichtel was on bass, Gerry Neiwood on flute and sax, Coleman Mellet, guitar, and Dave Tull on drums. Corey Allen was usually on keyboards but couldn't make the gig this time. We were a pretty close-knit band but we'd all end up even closer due to something the next day that would change our lives forever.

The band was slated to perform at an open-air concert, but beforehand we did the tourist thing going to ancient palaces and market places. In the States my girl had asked someone how to say a few pertinent phrases, such as, "where's the bathroom" and the like. This someone vowed that everyone spoke English so it wasn't necessary. Very untrue, ladies and gentlemen. So, I'm drinking a beer or two in Seoul and now we're trying to mime "where's the bathroom?" We tried just about every gesture short of being downright vulgar. The confused waitress finally smiled. Mission accomplished, we'd gotten our point across at last. She disappeared in the back and then returned with a pitcher of water. I guess we hadn't done such a great job after all. Somehow or another we found the right door after walking into the kitchen and then the broom closet. Next time around, remind me to get a phrase book.

Back at the hotel, I was getting ready for the gig and now, you know, I'm a media junkie so the TV was on. CNN to be exact. The date was September 12th but just remember that we were in Korea with that thirteen-hour difference. In disbelief and horror we watched the World Trade Center tower fall. It was totally surreal. We could hardly believe our eyes. Then we saw the plane literally dissect the second tower. I won't go into any more detail because it's a most terrible and painful memory for everyone. We first assumed it was an accident, then, we feared it was the beginning of World War III. Mel ran into

Chazz Frichtel's room to use his laptop to contact our New York friends and family to see if they were all right. You have to remember that no one back then had laptops, but Chazz was always a bit ahead of the time with technology.

A curfew was immediately imposed in Seoul. Not really knowing what was going on, we were thinking that there might be some kind of hostility towards Americans in Korea, too.

Chuck's friend, who also accompanied us on the trip, happened to be a professional bodyguard, master driver, and sharpshooter. I think she was saying that she'd driven for some high-level generals in Europe and could maneuver around anything. And yeah, that's right, I did say, she. She drove us to the venue and barricaded all but one green room door with chairs. During the concert, she scanned the audience from the right wings and told my girl to keep a watchful eye from the left looking for anything or anyone suspicious. We all agreed with Chuck's wife, Rosie, who said, "Now that's the kind of woman you want around."

Chuck started off the set with "Feels So Good," transitioned into "America the Beautiful," and then back into "Feels so Good." It felt so patriotic and we were all so moved. He continued with his many hits. The audience loved him, and guess what? Nothing terrible happened, but man, it was such a difficult night for us all. We could only imagine how rough it was for everyone back home.

The international airports had all closed down and we were stranded in Korea. We felt helpless and confused, longing for the safety of family and friends, and much relieved when the airports opened up days later. Our next destination was Hawaii to play at a jazz festival on The Big Island. Now, I wasn't feeling great. We were walking into the airport and I could hardly stand up anymore. My girl went to get me assistance but because we couldn't read Korean, she ended up in a restricted area. Some military official apprehended her with his bayonet and took her passport away. I don't know exactly how it all worked out, but she ended up with a wheel chair for me and we got on that flight to Honolulu.

It was so great to be back on American soil. Hawaii would have definitely been the better place to be stranded and nothing like a bit of paradise to get you feeling better. We were staying at a place where you actually rode a gondola down to your hotel room past meridians of exotic flowers and birds. The concert we were to play at was again open air but no matter how beautiful Hawaii was, we still couldn't get those ugly images out of our minds. Before the festival concert started, we all had a moment of silence on stage, then Chuck played "Taps." It was an intense concert for us. We played our hearts out and dedicated our music to the many who perished.

A few days later, we were flying back to New York and didn't know what to expect. Our flight was with American and we all wished it weren't, as they had been the ill-fated airline. Before boarding, the airlines confiscated my tuning fork as they considered it a potential weapon. Let's just say they were being extremely cautious. Once in the air, even the stewardesses admitted to being nervous. There was a rustling from behind the curtain that separated first class from coach. My girl and I looked at one another, and then at the two bottles of red wine we were bringing back to New York. We had decided in advance we'd smash it over someone's head if there were anyone threatening onboard. It's much easier to be valiant in fantasy, so thank God, the rustling was merely the steward coming through with magazines. For the rest of the flight people were eying each other. Maybe they were looking for the strongest person to come to their rescue if something went down. Maybe they were checking out anyone who looked suspicious, I know we were. Racial profiling was going to go to a whole other level and those great days of being on tour, my friend, would never be the same.

We arrived in New York safely. Even though Mel and I lived uptown, we noticed that there was soot on our floor that had sifted through our slightly open window. There must have been a whole lot of that in the air to have reached our place miles away. In days to come, New Yorkers seemed more thoughtful. There was a sense of camaraderie and compassion. That, however, didn't last long and we were happy to go out on tour again, this time with David Sanborn.

17.

Dave Sanborn

When I think about it, I'd been playing with Dave for almost two decades. We had been to Japan numerous times and we were going again. The Japanese really liked their jazz and we loved them for liking us.

If you've ever flown from New York to Tokyo, you know it's a good twelve-hour flight. I must say that JAL is a great airline, but those seats are definitely not made for a Harlem-born and bred behind like mine. It's not an easy ride, but nothing that a Tylenol PM couldn't fix. I was eager to show my girl Japan and was looking forward to our usual gigs at the Blue Note. I admit, the Japanese are the world's greatest imitators and their musicians can really play jazz. What a great culture, too. It has that unique mixture of ancient and contemporary with such polite people.

On a previous tour, I'd met up with my musician friend who lived near Tokyo. We had stopped to get gas and it happened to be on the late side. The attendants were just closing up and weren't too happy to service us. They smiled in our face but said all sorts of nasty things about us in Japanese like, "Go home you Black, pain in the ass, mother fuckers." My friend had married a Japanese woman and was quite fluent in the language. We just let them carry on calling us every name in the book. Then he answered them back in Japanese. It definitely took them by surprise. Ordinarily though, we were treated in Japan with great respect, or hey, maybe we just thought we were!

On this trip we were going to perform at the Blue Note in Fukuoka and then in Tokyo. Now, I like Tokyo but Fukuoka is a great city, reminding me of a Japanese East Village. The Blue Note there is actually walking distance from the hotel so it's great to stroll down those lively streets on the way to the gig. Lots of young kids had dyed their hair red, and wore American fashions. They rode their motorbikes down the streets and nobody screamed, "Hey, get the f out of the way." Nice change.

While my girl and I were walking around, a guy stopped us and pointed to a piece of paper he was holding. We were finally able to decipher, "Donaldo Alias San." He actually wanted my autograph. It was like when Grace Jones recognized me in the airport. That sort of thing really knocks me out. I always consider that an honor.

So, no sooner did we get off the plane, then we were rehearsing. Talk about tired, ladies and gentlemen. We were all a bit fried from traveling and jet lag hadn't even had the chance to set in.

But the music was going to be outstanding. Dave had Ricky Peterson on keyboards and his playing is so melodic. He can sing his ass off too. Gene Lake is such a powerful drummer and Dean Brown, our consummate guitarist, the audience loves as much as we do. We all love Nicky Moroch too. His guitar playing is so fast and furious and though Nicky wasn't on this gig, he's with Dave more often than not these days. Then there was our fierce bass player, Richard Patterson. The guys can all really play and have been with Sanborn for so long it's like second nature. Dave's been making his mark for decades with his alto sax playing and the many Grammys, platinum and gold albums didn't hurt his popularity either. He's really in demand in Japan and plays sets that include those wonderful Marcus Miller tunes like "Camel Island" and "Chicago Song" along with Dave's bests and other composers too. Needless to say, we all could do without "Spooky," no offense to anyone.

This tour, I took a solo on the bass kalimba and udu, while chanting to the Orishas, and got the audience to join in. It's so great to see the Japanese, who are generally more contained, get really involved. I walked onto the floor and played on people's water glasses with my sticks, then on my girl's high-heeled shoes. At the end of the set, the joke with the band is that I'm on the bus before the last string on the guitar finishes resonating. True enough. Me and my girl are the first ones out. Mel placed a towel around my neck 'cause I was sweating like crazy and my eyes were once again too bloodshot. She was worrying about me again, but when I play, I play hard and there's no holding back.

The Blue Note was sold out every show and the band was on fire every night. During the days, we had such a great time too. Our music producer friend, Yoko Yamabe, took us around and showed us some great places. What hospitality. Thank you, Yoko San, even if our sushi did cost almost two hundred bucks.

Now, I'm a big fan of Sumo, too. It's such an interesting tradition with the wrestlers slapping their *mawashis* and eating that nutritional porridge that makes their voices low and puts on the weight. I wonder what the hell is in that. During the afternoons, the band members would be in their hotel rooms watching the matches on TV. We'd be calling each other on the phone for all the great takedowns, like football fans. I have to admit, it was hard to tear myself away from the TV even to make it to the gig. Of course, once we were playing, that magic I always talk about sets in. As usual, it was an amazing two weeks that just flew by.

After the tour, the Blue Note management accompanied us to the airport to see us off. They bowed goodbye, so we did, too. They bowed a little lower and to keep up with being polite, we did the same. It must have been a strange looking scene to see everyone walking in reverse. Then they continued to walk backwards bowing even lower. Now I'm a tall guy, so that's as far as it could go, but all I can say is, what a great send-off.

Next on the itinerary was South Africa and Brazil. Though I'm a real private guy, I'll tell you that I was hitting some tough times. I was in and out of emergency rooms having health challenges. My girl was doing the Florence Nightingale thing with me. Not fun, I'm sure of

96

that. Let's just say that we never made it to those places I mentioned. Things were slowing down, and for necessary reasons. I entertained retiring to St. Maarten just to swim in the sea as my grandmother did, enjoying a simpler life. But if you remember, Nina said, "Drums are like your heartbeat and you know you can't live without your heartbeat." I don't think I could ever exist without playing music.

Epilogue

Perhaps you've wondered what would possess someone to beat on a drum with their hands? It's a strange instrument, I must say. In some ways it's really masochistic, but I have had this absolute love for percussion. It's been a gift and there was no choice in the matter. It was just something I had to do. Now you know that beating on the congas brought me from playing in the streets of Harlem to performing with Miles Davis.

Fate definitely had its way, and led me into this fifty-year career playing with so many greats that I couldn't even name them all for you. What an honor it's been. It's brought me around the world and gave me a life I never expected. Somehow, with a little luck, I was able to satisfy my creative dreams and hey, they even paid me for it. And believe me, it all started with those pots and pans.

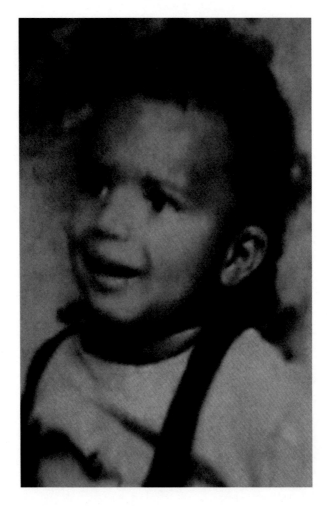

Photos credit : Melanie Futorian and courtesy of Kimmi Alias and Gene Perla

Art work by Yoko Yamabe

Photo by Rosemary Andress-Sanborn

About the Author

Melanie Futorian has been a feature writer for *Allaboutjazz.com*, where she had her own column, "Cymbalism." Her articles have also appeared in *Dance Teacher Magazine, Dance Insider,* and United Nations Society of Writers publication.

She has been a camerawoman for the United Nations, CNN News, FOX News Channel, MTV, SNY. In addition, Melanie has photographed for UNESCO, UNCA, the Martha Graham Dance Company, the Limon Dance Company, Paul Taylor Dance Company, Mark Morris Dance Group, STREB and major jazz musicians.

Her photography was exhibited at The Jakmel Gallery in Miami, and can be seen in *Allaboutjazz.com*, as well as David Sanborn's CD liner, "Time and the River."

Ms. Futorian was also a professional dancer for various New York companies such as Forces of Nature, Manhattan Opera Company, Haitian American Dance Theater, and Ballet America. Some of her teaching and choreography includes Alvin Ailey's summer program, M.I.T.'s Dance Troupe, Fordham University, Harlem Village Academy and the movie "Creeporia."

Acknowledgments

Special thanks to

Sara, Elliot and Andrea Baker and Kalie Rae

for your enormous support and incredible editing!

Many thanks to George Libbares for your expertise

To Yoko Yamabe for your amazing, creative art work!

Much love to my family

and to my special friends, who know who they are.

Don's journal entry

Made in the USA
San Bernardino, CA
02 May 2017